EPIC FAILS AND EPIC WINS

A JOURNAL

CHRONICLE BOOKS
SAN FRANCISCO

W9-CEE-139

ISBN 978-1-4521-1079-0

Manufactured in China
Design by Kelly Abeln

Chronicle Books publishes distinctive books and gifts.
From award-winning children's titles, best-selling
cookbooks, and eclectic pop culture to acclaimed
works of art and design, stationery, and journals, we
craft publishing that's instantly recognizable for its
spirit and creativity. Enjoy our publishing and become
part of our community at www.chroniclebooks.com.

10 9 8 7 6 5 4 3 2 1

Chronicle Books LLC
680 Second Street
San Francisco, CA 94107
www.chroniclebooks.com

IT ALWAYS STARTS OUT SO INNOCENTLY.

You're having a perfectly fine day, doing something totally normal like filming yourself performing the "Single Ladies" dance in a one-piece thong and a cowboy hat, and the next thing you know you're face-planting on the carpet, your roommate's uploading it to Facebook, and suddenly your butt is all over the Internet. Welcome to the world of the EPIC FAIL (or, if you *like* how you look facedown in a thong, the EPIC WIN).

It's a tradition with a long, proud history. There have been big failures and big successes since the dawn of man, and if anything, they used to be even bigger. Epic wins were, well, actual epics (*Beowulf* equals WIN). Epic fails tended to involve planet-wide destruction (dinosaurs equal FAIL). As the years passed, there were more wins (fire; walking upright; the wheel), and more fails (the Crusades; the Inquisition; bubonic plague). In the 1990s, *America's Funniest Home Videos* brought the fail to a bigger audience, letting you share with the entire nation that home movie of your dad taking a wiffle bat to the crotch. A few years later, the Internet came along, letting you share the same movie with the whole *world*. Now epic fails and epic wins happen at lightning speed, and there's always someone with a smartphone nearby to film the whole thing and post it to YouTube.

But how to keep track of all these fails and wins?

You could tweet all the gory details, but sometimes you just want to keep them to yourself. You need a more old-school method, and a gratitude journal won't cut it. Your life is not like that. Your life is like accidentally sending a sext to your mom, or crashing a car into a mini-mart, or landing a perfect dismount in a public fountain.

Fortunately, the EPIC FAILS and EPIC WINS Journal is here to help you chronicle all that.

Whether you are the responsible party or the witness of an epic fail or win, you can now keep a record of all the hilarious details. This journal will help you remember your personal highs and lows, give you the tools to evaluate them for epicness, and help you learn how to win and fail even more epically.

Best of all, the journal will help you learn how to turn all those tragic fails into massive wins. It _is_ possible. Sometimes a fail is so incredibly epic that it crosses the boundary into win territory. And just by its sheer amazingness, the epic fail becomes immortalized as a win. In fact, the whole concept of the FAIL may be the best example. FAIL is believed to derive from the very poor Japanese-to-English translation in an old arcade game called Blazing Star, in which losers were berated, "You fail it! Your skill is not enough! See you next time! Bye-bye!" The clunky term "You fail it!" became an Internet taunt that eventually truncated into FAIL . . . turning a translation fail into a great big WIN.

So grab your journal, your pen, and your one-piece thong. You've got a lot to do, and it's all going to be EPIC.

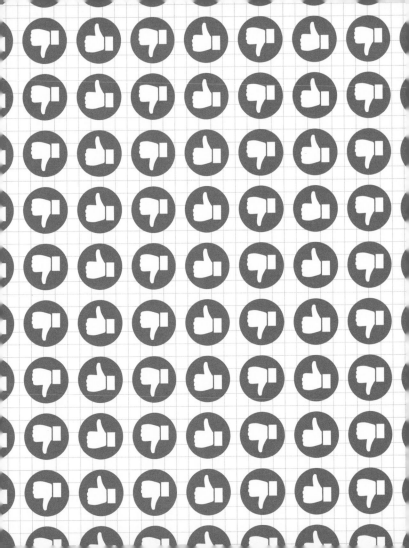

TODAY WAS:

- ❏ Okay
- ❏ Good
- ❏ Awesome
- ❏ Epic
- ❏ Lame
- ❏ Bad
- ❏ Super crappy
- ❏ Worst. Day. Ever.

_____

DATE

👎 TODAY'S FAIL:

- ❏ Average
- ❏ EPIC
- ❏ Super Mega EPIC
- ❏ So EPIC it's a WIN

❏ I / ❏ Who?_____ **DID WHAT?**_____

_____

_____

WHY?
- ❏ Totally meant to do that
- ❏ Trying to impress someone
- ❏ Other_____
- ❏ Drunk
- ❏ Just a jackass

WILL THE LOSERS INVOLVED HAVE TO:

❏ Go to the hospital? ❏ Move to a new town? ❏ Get plastic surgery?
❏ Get therapy? ❏ Other_____

LESSON LEARNED:_____

_____

❏ NEVER again ❏ Maybe again ❏ Do again at first opportunity

👍 TODAY'S WIN:

☐ Above Average   ☐ Massive   ☐ EPIC   ☐ Super Mega EPIC

☐ I / ☐ Who?_____ **DID WHAT?**_____

_____

_____

WHY? ☐ Totally awesome   ☐ Preparation
       ☐ Deserved it   ☐ Dumb luck
       ☐ Other_____

DID THE WIN RESULT IN A:

☐ New nickname?   ☐ Hookup?   ☐ Trophy?
☐ Arrest?   ☐ Other_____

ALL HAIL_____, **RULER OF**_____!
        (winner's name)   (today's win)

Schadenfreude is the German word for the feeling of pleasure we get from another's misfortune, and it's what's behind our enjoyment of the **EPIC FAIL.** There is no German word for pleasure in another's win.

👍 TODAY'S WIN:

❏ Above Average   ❏ Massive   ❏ EPIC   ❏ Super Mega EPIC

❏ I / ❏ Who?_____ **DID WHAT?**_____

_____

_____

WHY? ❏ Totally awesome   ❏ Preparation
          ❏ Deserved it   ❏ Dumb luck
          ❏ Other_____

DID THE WIN RESULT IN A:

❏ New nickname?   ❏ Hookup?   ❏ Trophy?
❏ Arrest?   ❏ Other _____

ALL HAIL_____, **RULER OF**_____!
     (winner's name)   (today's win)

FAIL⇨WIN: In 1930, Ruth Wakefield was making a batch of chocolate cookies but didn't have time to melt and blend chocolate into the dough. So she threw in some chocolate chunks, figuring they'd melt into the dough in the oven. They didn't, and the chocolate chip cookie was born. **WIN!**

TODAY WAS:

- ❏ Okay
- ❏ Good
- ❏ Awesome
- ❏ Epic
- ❏ Lame
- ❏ Bad
- ❏ Super crappy
- ❏ Worst. Day. Ever.

_____
DATE

👎 TODAY'S FAIL:

❏ Average   ❏ EPIC   ❏ Super Mega EPIC   ❏ So EPIC it's a WIN

❏ I / ❏ Who?_____ **DID WHAT?**_____

_____

_____

WHY?
- ❏ Totally meant to do that
- ❏ Trying to impress someone
- ❏ Other_____
- ❏ Drunk
- ❏ Just a jackass

WILL THE LOSERS INVOLVED HAVE TO:

❏ Go to the hospital?   ❏ Move to a new town?   ❏ Get plastic surgery?
❏ Get therapy?   ❏ Other_____

LESSON LEARNED: _____

_____

❏ NEVER again   ❏ Maybe again   ❏ Do again at first opportunity

👍 TODAY'S WIN:

☐ Above Average   ☐ Massive   ☐ EPIC   ☐ Super Mega EPIC

☐ I / ☐ Who?_____ **DID WHAT?**_____

_____

_____

WHY?   ☐ Totally awesome   ☐ Preparation
      ☐ Deserved it   ☐ Dumb luck
      ☐ Other_____

DID THE WIN RESULT IN A:

☐ New nickname?   ☐ Hookup?   ☐ Trophy?
☐ Arrest?   ☐ Other_____

ALL HAIL_____, **RULER OF**_____!
        (winner's name)   (today's win)

If you're racking up a lot more **FAILs** than **WINs**, you may just need to
get more sleep. Being awake for twenty hours is equivalent to drinking
more than four beers. And a lot less fun.

TODAY WAS:

- ❏ Okay
- ❏ Good
- ❏ Awesome
- ❏ Epic
- ❏ Lame
- ❏ Bad
- ❏ Super crappy
- ❏ Worst. Day. Ever.

_____
DATE

👎 TODAY'S FAIL:

- ❏ Average
- ❏ EPIC
- ❏ Super Mega EPIC
- ❏ So EPIC it's a WIN

❏ I / ❏ Who?_____ **DID WHAT?**_____

_____

_____

WHY?
- ❏ Totally meant to do that
- ❏ Trying to impress someone
- ❏ Other_____
- ❏ Drunk
- ❏ Just a jackass

WILL THE LOSERS INVOLVED HAVE TO:

- ❏ Go to the hospital?
- ❏ Get therapy?
- ❏ Move to a new town?
- ❏ Other_____
- ❏ Get plastic surgery?

LESSON LEARNED:_____

_____

❏ NEVER again ❏ Maybe again ❏ Do again at first opportunity

👍 TODODAY'S WIN:

☐ Above Average   ☐ Massive   ☐ EPIC   ☐ Super Mega EPIC

☐ I / ☐ Who?_____ **DID WHAT?**_____

_____

_____

WHY?
☐ Totally awesome   ☐ Preparation
☐ Deserved it   ☐ Dumb luck
☐ Other_____

DID THE WIN RESULT IN A:

☐ New nickname?   ☐ Hookup?   ☐ Trophy?
☐ Arrest?   ☐ Other_____

ALL HAIL_____, RULER OF_____!
         (winner's name)   (today's win)

> **FAIL⇨WIN:** Swiss engineer George de Mestral came home from a walk and found a mess of burrs stuck to his clothes. He examined the burrs under a microscope and thought he might be able to reproduce their stickiness for good. The result? Velcro. **WIN!**

TODAY WAS:

- ❏ Okay
- ❏ Good
- ❏ Awesome
- ❏ Epic
- ❏ Lame
- ❏ Bad
- ❏ Super crappy
- ❏ Worst. Day. Ever.

_____
DATE

👎 TODAY'S FAIL:

- ❏ Average
- ❏ EPIC
- ❏ Super Mega EPIC
- ❏ So EPIC it's a WIN

❏ I / ❏ Who?_____ **DID WHAT?**_____

_____

_____

WHY?
- ❏ Totally meant to do that
- ❏ Trying to impress someone
- ❏ Other_____
- ❏ Drunk
- ❏ Just a jackass

WILL THE LOSERS INVOLVED HAVE TO:

- ❏ Go to the hospital?
- ❏ Get therapy?
- ❏ Move to a new town?
- ❏ Other_____
- ❏ Get plastic surgery?

LESSON LEARNED:_____

_____

❏ NEVER again ❏ Maybe again ❏ Do again at first opportunity

👍 TODAY'S WIN:

❏ Above Average   ❏ Massive   ❏ EPIC   ❏ Super Mega EPIC

❏ I / ❏ Who?_____ **DID WHAT?**_____

_____

_____

WHY?   ❏ Totally awesome   ❏ Preparation
           ❏ Deserved it   ❏ Dumb luck
           ❏ Other_____

DID THE WIN RESULT IN A:

❏ New nickname?   ❏ Hookup?   ❏ Trophy?
❏ Arrest?   ❏ Other_____

ALL HAIL _____ , **RULER OF**_____ !
             (winner's name)   (today's win)

> "Success is the ability to go from one failure to another with no loss
> of enthusiasm."
>
> **—WINSTON CHURCHILL**

TODAY WAS:

❏ Okay ❏ Lame
❏ Good ❏ Bad
❏ Awesome ❏ Super crappy
❏ Epic ❏ Worst. Day. Ever.

DATE

👎 TODAY'S FAIL:

❏ Average ❏ EPIC ❏ Super Mega EPIC ❏ So EPIC it's a WIN

❏ I / ❏ Who?_____ **DID WHAT?**_____

_____

_____

WHY?
❏ Totally meant to do that ❏ Drunk
❏ Trying to impress someone ❏ Just a jackass
❏ Other_____

WILL THE LOSERS INVOLVED HAVE TO:

❏ Go to the hospital? ❏ Move to a new town? ❏ Get plastic surgery?
❏ Get therapy? ❏ Other_____

LESSON LEARNED:_____

_____

❏ NEVER again ❏ Maybe again ❏ Do again at first opportunity

👍 TODODAY'S WIN:

☐ Above Average ☐ Massive ☐ EPIC ☐ Super Mega EPIC

☐ I / ☐ Who?_____ **DID WHAT?**_____

_____

_____

WHY?
☐ Totally awesome ☐ Preparation
☐ Deserved it ☐ Dumb luck
☐ Other_____

DID THE WIN RESULT IN A:

☐ New nickname? ☐ Hookup? ☐ Trophy?
☐ Arrest? ☐ Other_____

ALL HAIL _____ , RULER OF_____ !
(winner's name)   (today's win)

FAIL⇨WIN: In 1943, a G.E. engineer named James Wright was conducting an experiment with boric acid and silicone oil that resulted in a useless blob of goo. Only it turned out not to be so useless after all. He'd invented Silly Putty. **WIN!**

TODAY WAS:

- ❏ Okay
- ❏ Good
- ❏ Awesome
- ❏ Epic
- ❏ Lame
- ❏ Bad
- ❏ Super crappy
- ❏ Worst. Day. Ever.

_____

DATE

👎 TODAY'S FAIL:

- ❏ Average
- ❏ EPIC
- ❏ Super Mega EPIC
- ❏ So EPIC it's a WIN

❏ I / ❏ Who?_____ **DID WHAT?**_____

_____

_____

WHY?
- ❏ Totally meant to do that
- ❏ Trying to impress someone
- ❏ Other_____
- ❏ Drunk
- ❏ Just a jackass

WILL THE LOSERS INVOLVED HAVE TO:

- ❏ Go to the hospital?
- ❏ Get therapy?
- ❏ Move to a new town?
- ❏ Other_____
- ❏ Get plastic surgery?

LESSON LEARNED:_____

_____

❏ NEVER again   ❏ Maybe again   ❏ Do again at first opportunity

👍 TODODAY'S WIN: ◀

☐ Above Average ☐ Massive ☐ EPIC ☐ Super Mega EPIC

☐ I / ☐ Who?_____ **DID WHAT?**_____

_____

_____

WHY? ☐ Totally awesome ☐ Preparation
☐ Deserved it ☐ Dumb luck
☐ Other_____

DID THE WIN RESULT IN A:

☐ New nickname? ☐ Hookup? ☐ Trophy?
☐ Arrest? ☐ Other_____

ALL HAIL_____, RULER OF_____!
(winner's name)   (today's win)

WIN/FAIL fact: The L to the forehead doesn't mean "loser" everywhere. In the Philippines, it's a political rallying gesture that means "Fight!" **WIN!**

TODAY WAS:

- ❏ Okay
- ❏ Good
- ❏ Awesome
- ❏ Epic
- ❏ Lame
- ❏ Bad
- ❏ Super crappy
- ❏ Worst. Day. Ever.

_____ DATE

👎 TODAY'S FAIL:

❏ Average ❏ EPIC ❏ Super Mega EPIC ❏ So EPIC it's a WIN

❏ I / ❏ Who?_____ **DID WHAT?**_____

_____

_____

WHY?
- ❏ Totally meant to do that
- ❏ Trying to impress someone
- ❏ Other_____
- ❏ Drunk
- ❏ Just a jackass

WILL THE LOSERS INVOLVED HAVE TO:

❏ Go to the hospital? ❏ Move to a new town? ❏ Get plastic surgery?
❏ Get therapy? ❏ Other_____

LESSON LEARNED: _____

_____

❏ NEVER again ❏ Maybe again ❏ Do again at first opportunity

👍 TODODAY'S WIN:

❏ Above Average ❏ Massive ❏ EPIC ❏ Super Mega EPIC

❏ I / ❏ Who?_____ **DID WHAT?**_____

_____

_____

WHY? ❏ Totally awesome ❏ Preparation
❏ Deserved it ❏ Dumb luck
❏ Other_____

DID THE WIN RESULT IN A:

❏ New nickname? ❏ Hookup? ❏ Trophy?
❏ Arrest? ❏ Other_____

ALL HAIL_____, RULER OF_____!
   (winner's name)   (today's win)

WIN/FAIL fact: The V for Victory sign does not mean "victory" everywhere.
In some countries, it means, "Up yours." **FAIL!**

TODAY WAS:

- ❏ Okay
- ❏ Good
- ❏ Awesome
- ❏ Epic
- ❏ Lame
- ❏ Bad
- ❏ Super crappy
- ❏ Worst. Day. Ever.

_____
DATE

👎 TODAY'S FAIL:

❏ Average   ❏ EPIC   ❏ Super Mega EPIC   ❏ So EPIC it's a WIN

❏ I / ❏ Who?_____ **DID WHAT?**_____

_____

_____

WHY?
- ❏ Totally meant to do that
- ❏ Trying to impress someone
- ❏ Other_____
- ❏ Drunk
- ❏ Just a jackass

WILL THE LOSERS INVOLVED HAVE TO:

❏ Go to the hospital?   ❏ Move to a new town?   ❏ Get plastic surgery?
❏ Get therapy?   ❏ Other_____

LESSON LEARNED: _____

_____

❏ NEVER again   ❏ Maybe again   ❏ Do again at first opportunity

👍 TODGY'S WIN:

☐ Above Average   ☐ Massive   ☐ EPIC   ☐ Super Mega EPIC

☐ I / ☐ Who?_____ **DID WHAT?**_____

_____

_____

WHY? ☐ Totally awesome   ☐ Preparation
        ☐ Deserved it   ☐ Dumb luck
        ☐ Other_____

DID THE WIN RESULT IN A:

☐ New nickname?   ☐ Hookup?   ☐ Trophy?
☐ Arrest?   ☐ Other_____

ALL HAIL _____ , RULER OF _____ !
     (winner's name)   (today's win)

Schadenfreude is the German word for the feeling of pleasure we get from another's misfortune, and it's what's behind our enjoyment of the **EPIC FAIL.** There is no German word for pleasure in another's win.

TODAY WAS:

❏ Okay   ❏ Lame
❏ Good   ❏ Bad
❏ Awesome   ❏ Super crappy
❏ Epic   ❏ Worst. Day. Ever.

_____
DATE

👎 TODAY'S FAIL:

❏ Average   ❏ EPIC   ❏ Super Mega EPIC   ❏ So EPIC it's a WIN

❏ I / ❏ Who?_____ **DID WHAT?**_____

_____

_____

WHY?   ❏ Totally meant to do that   ❏ Drunk
       ❏ Trying to impress someone   ❏ Just a jackass
       ❏ Other_____

WILL THE LOSERS INVOLVED HAVE TO:

❏ Go to the hospital?   ❏ Move to a new town?   ❏ Get plastic surgery?
❏ Get therapy?   ❏ Other_____

LESSON LEARNED: _____

_____

❏ NEVER again   ❏ Maybe again   ❏ Do again at first opportunity

👍 TODODAY'S WIN:

☐ Above Average   ☐ Massive   ☐ EPIC   ☐ Super Mega EPIC

☐ I / ☐ Who?_____ **DID WHAT?**_____

_____

_____

WHY? ☐ Totally awesome   ☐ Preparation
          ☐ Deserved it   ☐ Dumb luck
          ☐ Other_____

DID THE WIN RESULT IN A:

☐ New nickname?   ☐ Hookup?   ☐ Trophy?
☐ Arrest?   ☐ Other_____

ALL HAIL _____, RULER OF_____!
         (winner's name)   (today's win)

FAIL⇨WIN: In 1930, Ruth Wakefield was making a batch of chocolate cookies but didn't have time to melt and blend chocolate into the dough. So she threw in some chocolate chunks, figuring they'd melt into the dough in the oven. They didn't, and the chocolate chip cookie was born. **WIN!**

TODAY WAS:

❏ Okay ❏ Lame
❏ Good ❏ Bad
❏ Awesome ❏ Super crappy
❏ Epic ❏ Worst. Day. Ever.

_____
DATE

👎 TODAY'S FAIL:

❏ Average ❏ EPIC ❏ Super Mega EPIC ❏ So EPIC it's a WIN

❏ I / ❏ Who?_____ **DID WHAT?**_____

_____

_____

WHY? ❏ Totally meant to do that ❏ Drunk
❏ Trying to impress someone ❏ Just a jackass
❏ Other_____

WILL THE LOSERS INVOLVED HAVE TO:

❏ Go to the hospital? ❏ Move to a new town? ❏ Get plastic surgery?
❏ Get therapy? ❏ Other_____

LESSON LEARNED: _____

_____

❏ NEVER again ❏ Maybe again ❏ Do again at first opportunity

👍 TODAY'S WIN:

☐ Above Average ☐ Massive ☐ EPIC ☐ Super Mega EPIC

☐ I / ☐ Who?_____ **DID WHAT?**_____

_____

_____

WHY? ☐ Totally awesome ☐ Preparation
      ☐ Deserved it ☐ Dumb luck
      ☐ Other_____

DID THE WIN RESULT IN A:

☐ New nickname? ☐ Hookup? ☐ Trophy?
☐ Arrest? ☐ Other_____

ALL HAIL _____ , RULER OF _____ !
    (winner's name)   (today's win)

If you're racking up a lot more **FAILs** than **WINs**, you may just need to get more sleep. Being awake for twenty hours is equivalent to drinking more than four beers. And a lot less fun.

TODAY WAS:

❑ Okay   ❑ Lame
❑ Good   ❑ Bad
❑ Awesome   ❑ Super crappy   _____
❑ Epic   ❑ Worst. Day. Ever.   DATE

👎 TODAY'S FAIL:

❑ Average   ❑ EPIC   ❑ Super Mega EPIC   ❑ So EPIC it's a WIN

❑ I / ❑ Who?_____ **DID WHAT?**_____

_____

_____

WHY? ❑ Totally meant to do that   ❑ Drunk
       ❑ Trying to impress someone   ❑ Just a jackass
       ❑ Other_____

WILL THE LOSERS INVOLVED HAVE TO:

❑ Go to the hospital?   ❑ Move to a new town?   ❑ Get plastic surgery?
❑ Get therapy?   ❑ Other_____

LESSON LEARNED: _____

_____

❑ NEVER again   ❑ Maybe again   ❑ Do again at first opportunity

👍 TODODAY'S WIN:

☐ Above Average   ☐ Massive   ☐ EPIC   ☐ Super Mega EPIC

☐ I / ☐ Who?_____ **DID WHAT?**_____

_____

_____

WHY?   ☐ Totally awesome   ☐ Preparation

       ☐ Deserved it   ☐ Dumb luck

       ☐ Other_____

DID THE WIN RESULT IN A:

☐ New nickname?   ☐ Hookup?   ☐ Trophy?

☐ Arrest?   ☐ Other_____

ALL HAIL_____, **RULER OF**_____!

          (winner's name)   (today's win)

> **FAIL⇒WIN:** Swiss engineer George de Mestral came home from a walk and found a mess of burrs stuck to his clothes. He examined the burrs under a microscope and thought he might be able to reproduce their stickiness for good. The result? Velcro. **WIN!**

TODAY WAS:

❑ Okay   ❑ Lame
❑ Good   ❑ Bad
❑ Awesome   ❑ Super crappy   **DATE**
❑ Epic   ❑ Worst. Day. Ever.

👎 TODAY'S FAIL:

❑ Average   ❑ EPIC   ❑ Super Mega EPIC   ❑ So EPIC it's a WIN

❑ I / ❑ Who?_____ **DID WHAT?**_____

_____

_____

WHY?   ❑ Totally meant to do that   ❑ Drunk
       ❑ Trying to impress someone   ❑ Just a jackass
       ❑ Other_____

WILL THE LOSERS INVOLVED HAVE TO:

❑ Go to the hospital?   ❑ Move to a new town?   ❑ Get plastic surgery?
❑ Get therapy?   ❑ Other_____

LESSON LEARNED: _____

_____

❑ NEVER again   ❑ Maybe again   ❑ Do again at first opportunity

👍 TODAY'S WIN:

☐ Above Average   ☐ Massive   ☐ EPIC   ☐ Super Mega EPIC

☐ I / ☐ Who?_____ **DID WHAT?**_____

_____

_____

WHY?   ☐ Totally awesome   ☐ Preparation
          ☐ Deserved it   ☐ Dumb luck
          ☐ Other_____

DID THE WIN RESULT IN A:

☐ New nickname?   ☐ Hookup?   ☐ Trophy?
☐ Arrest?   ☐ Other_____

ALL HAIL _____, RULER OF _____!
(winner's name)   (today's win)

> *"Success is the ability to go from one failure to another with no loss of enthusiasm."*
>
> **—WINSTON CHURCHILL**

TODAY WAS:

❑ Okay   ❑ Lame
❑ Good   ❑ Bad
❑ Awesome   ❑ Super crappy   _____
❑ Epic   ❑ Worst. Day. Ever.   DATE

👎 TODAY'S FAIL:

❑ Average   ❑ EPIC   ❑ Super Mega EPIC   ❑ So EPIC it's a WIN

❑ I / ❑ Who?_____ **DID WHAT?**_____

_____

_____

WHY?   ❑ Totally meant to do that   ❑ Drunk
       ❑ Trying to impress someone   ❑ Just a jackass
       ❑ Other_____

WILL THE LOSERS INVOLVED HAVE TO:

❑ Go to the hospital?   ❑ Move to a new town?   ❑ Get plastic surgery?
❑ Get therapy?   ❑ Other_____

LESSON LEARNED:_____

_____

❑ NEVER again   ❑ Maybe again   ❑ Do again at first opportunity

👍 TODAY'S WIN:

☐ Above Average   ☐ Massive   ☐ EPIC   ☐ Super Mega EPIC

☐ I / ☐ Who?_____ **DID WHAT?**_____

_____

_____

WHY?   ☐ Totally awesome   ☐ Preparation
          ☐ Deserved it   ☐ Dumb luck
          ☐ Other_____

DID THE WIN RESULT IN A:

☐ New nickname?   ☐ Hookup?   ☐ Trophy?
☐ Arrest?   ☐ Other_____

ALL HAIL _____, **RULER OF**_____!
              (winner's name)   (today's win)

FAIL⇨WIN: In 1943, a G.E. engineer named James Wright was
conducting an experiment with boric acid and silicone oil that resulted
in a useless blob of goo. Only it turned out not to be so useless after all.
He'd invented Silly Putty. **WIN!**

TODAY WAS:

❏ Okay ❏ Lame
❏ Good ❏ Bad
❏ Awesome ❏ Super crappy
❏ Epic ❏ Worst. Day. Ever.

_____
DATE

👎 TODAY'S FAIL:

❏ Average ❏ EPIC ❏ Super Mega EPIC ❏ So EPIC it's a WIN

❏ I / ❏ Who?_____ **DID WHAT?**_____

_____

_____

WHY? ❏ Totally meant to do that ❏ Drunk
❏ Trying to impress someone ❏ Just a jackass
❏ Other_____

WILL THE LOSERS INVOLVED HAVE TO:

❏ Go to the hospital? ❏ Move to a new town? ❏ Get plastic surgery?
❏ Get therapy? ❏ Other_____

LESSON LEARNED:_____

_____

❏ NEVER again ❏ Maybe again ❏ Do again at first opportunity

👍 TODAY'S WIN:

☐ Above Average ☐ Massive ☐ EPIC ☐ Super Mega EPIC

☐ I / ☐ Who?_____ **DID WHAT?**_____

_____

_____

WHY? ☐ Totally awesome ☐ Preparation
☐ Deserved it ☐ Dumb luck
☐ Other_____

DID THE WIN RESULT IN A:

☐ New nickname? ☐ Hookup? ☐ Trophy?
☐ Arrest? ☐ Other_____

ALL HAIL_____, RULER OF_____!
(winner's name) (today's win)

WIN/FAIL fact: The L to the forehead doesn't mean "loser" everywhere. In the Philippines, it's a political rallying gesture that means "Fight!" **WIN!**

TODAY WAS:

❏ Okay   ❏ Lame
❏ Good   ❏ Bad
❏ Awesome ❏ Super crappy   _____
❏ Epic   ❏ Worst. Day. Ever.   DATE

👎 TODAY'S FAIL:

❏ Average   ❏ EPIC   ❏ Super Mega EPIC   ❏ So EPIC it's a WIN

❏ I / ❏ Who?_____ **DID WHAT?**_____

_____

_____

WHY? ❏ Totally meant to do that   ❏ Drunk
      ❏ Trying to impress someone   ❏ Just a jackass
      ❏ Other_____

WILL THE LOSERS INVOLVED HAVE TO:

❏ Go to the hospital? ❏ Move to a new town? ❏ Get plastic surgery?
❏ Get therapy?   ❏ Other_____

LESSON LEARNED: _____

_____

❏ NEVER again ❏ Maybe again ❏ Do again at first opportunity

👍 TODODAY'S WIN:

☐ Above Average   ☐ Massive   ☐ EPIC   ☐ Super Mega EPIC

☐ I / ☐ Who?_____ **DID WHAT?**_____

_____

_____

WHY? ☐ Totally awesome   ☐ Preparation
          ☐ Deserved it   ☐ Dumb luck
          ☐ Other_____

DID THE WIN RESULT IN A:

☐ New nickname?   ☐ Hookup?   ☐ Trophy?
☐ Arrest?   ☐ Other_____

ALL HAIL _____, RULER OF_____!
            (winner's name)   (today's win)

WIN/FAIL fact: The V for Victory sign does not mean "victory" everywhere.
In some countries, it means, "Up yours." **FAIL!**

TODAY WAS:
- ❏ Okay
- ❏ Good
- ❏ Awesome
- ❏ Epic
- ❏ Lame
- ❏ Bad
- ❏ Super crappy
- ❏ Worst. Day. Ever.

_____
DATE

👎 TODAY'S FAIL:

❏ Average ❏ EPIC ❏ Super Mega EPIC ❏ So EPIC it's a WIN

❏ I / ❏ Who?_____ **DID WHAT?**_____

_____

_____

WHY?
- ❏ Totally meant to do that
- ❏ Trying to impress someone
- ❏ Other_____
- ❏ Drunk
- ❏ Just a jackass

WILL THE LOSERS INVOLVED HAVE TO:

❏ Go to the hospital? ❏ Move to a new town? ❏ Get plastic surgery?
❏ Get therapy? ❏ Other_____

LESSON LEARNED: _____

_____

❏ NEVER again ❏ Maybe again ❏ Do again at first opportunity

👍 TODAY'S WIN:

❏ Above Average ❏ Massive ❏ EPIC ❏ Super Mega EPIC

❏ I / ❏ Who?_____ **DID WHAT?**_____

_____

_____

WHY? ❏ Totally awesome ❏ Preparation
❏ Deserved it ❏ Dumb luck
❏ Other_____

DID THE WIN RESULT IN A:

❏ New nickname? ❏ Hookup? ❏ Trophy?
❏ Arrest? ❏ Other_____

ALL HAIL_____, RULER OF_____!
　　　　　　(winner's name)　　　　　　　　　　(today's win)

Schadenfreude is the German word for the feeling of pleasure we get from another's misfortune, and it's what's behind our enjoyment of the **EPIC FAIL.** There is no German word for pleasure in another's win.

TODAY WAS:

❏ Okay   ❏ Lame
❏ Good   ❏ Bad
❏ Awesome   ❏ Super crappy   DATE
❏ Epic   ❏ Worst. Day. Ever.

👎 TODAY'S FAIL:

❏ Average   ❏ EPIC   ❏ Super Mega EPIC   ❏ So EPIC it's a WIN

❏ I / ❏ Who?_____ **DID WHAT?**_____

_____

_____

WHY? ❏ Totally meant to do that   ❏ Drunk
       ❏ Trying to impress someone   ❏ Just a jackass
       ❏ Other_____

WILL THE LOSERS INVOLVED HAVE TO:

❏ Go to the hospital?   ❏ Move to a new town?   ❏ Get plastic surgery?
❏ Get therapy?   ❏ Other_____

LESSON LEARNED: _____

_____

❏ NEVER again   ❏ Maybe again   ❏ Do again at first opportunity

👍 TODAY'S WIN:

☐ Above Average   ☐ Massive   ☐ EPIC   ☐ Super Mega EPIC

☐ I / ☐ Who?_____ **DID WHAT?**_____

_____

_____

WHY? ☐ Totally awesome   ☐ Preparation
         ☐ Deserved it   ☐ Dumb luck
         ☐ Other_____

DID THE WIN RESULT IN A:

☐ New nickname?   ☐ Hookup?   ☐ Trophy?
☐ Arrest?   ☐ Other_____

ALL HAIL _____ , RULER OF_____ !
           (winner's name)   (today's win)

FAIL⇨WIN: In 1930, Ruth Wakefield was making a batch of chocolate cookies but didn't have time to melt and blend chocolate into the dough. So she threw in some chocolate chunks, figuring they'd melt into the dough in the oven. They didn't, and the chocolate chip cookie was born. **WIN!**

TODAY WAS:

- ❏ Okay
- ❏ Good
- ❏ Awesome
- ❏ Epic
- ❏ Lame
- ❏ Bad
- ❏ Super crappy
- ❏ Worst. Day. Ever.

_____
DATE

👎 TODAY'S FAIL:

❏ Average   ❏ EPIC   ❏ Super Mega EPIC   ❏ So EPIC it's a WIN

❏ I / ❏ Who?_____ **DID WHAT?**_____

_____

_____

WHY?
- ❏ Totally meant to do that
- ❏ Trying to impress someone
- ❏ Other_____
- ❏ Drunk
- ❏ Just a jackass

WILL THE LOSERS INVOLVED HAVE TO:

❏ Go to the hospital? ❏ Move to a new town? ❏ Get plastic surgery?
❏ Get therapy?   ❏ Other_____

LESSON LEARNED: _____

_____

❏ NEVER again   ❏ Maybe again   ❏ Do again at first opportunity

👍 TODEY'S WIN:

☐ Above Average   ☐ Massive   ☐ EPIC   ☐ Super Mega EPIC

☐ I / ☐ Who?_____ **DID WHAT?**_____

_____

_____

WHY?   ☐ Totally awesome   ☐ Preparation
☐ Deserved it   ☐ Dumb luck
☐ Other_____

DID THE WIN RESULT IN A:

☐ New nickname?   ☐ Hookup?   ☐ Trophy?
☐ Arrest?   ☐ Other_____

ALL HAIL _____, RULER OF_____ !
　　　　　(winner's name)　　　　　　　　　　　(today's win)

If you're racking up a lot more **FAILs** than **WINs**, you may just need to get more sleep. Being awake for twenty hours is equivalent to drinking more than four beers. And a lot less fun.

TODAY WAS:

❏ Okay   ❏ Lame
❏ Good   ❏ Bad
❏ Awesome   ❏ Super crappy
❏ Epic   ❏ Worst. Day. Ever.

_____
DATE

👎 **TODAY'S FAIL:**

❏ Average   ❏ EPIC   ❏ Super Mega EPIC   ❏ So EPIC it's a WIN

❏ I / ❏ Who?_____ **DID WHAT?**_____

_____

_____

WHY?   ❏ Totally meant to do that   ❏ Drunk
❏ Trying to impress someone   ❏ Just a jackass
❏ Other_____

WILL THE LOSERS INVOLVED HAVE TO:

❏ Go to the hospital?   ❏ Move to a new town?   ❏ Get plastic surgery?
❏ Get therapy?   ❏ Other_____

LESSON LEARNED:_____

_____

❏ NEVER again   ❏ Maybe again   ❏ Do again at first opportunity

👍 TODODAY'S WIN:

☐ Above Average ☐ Massive ☐ EPIC ☐ Super Mega EPIC

☐ I / ☐ Who?_____ **DID WHAT?**_____

_____

_____

WHY? ☐ Totally awesome   ☐ Preparation
          ☐ Deserved it   ☐ Dumb luck
          ☐ Other_____

DID THE WIN RESULT IN A:

☐ New nickname?   ☐ Hookup?   ☐ Trophy?
☐ Arrest?   ☐ Other_____

ALL HAIL _____ , RULER OF_____ !
          (winner's name)   (today's win)

FAIL⇨WIN: Swiss engineer George de Mestral came home from a walk and found a mess of burrs stuck to his clothes. He examined the burrs under a microscope and thought he might be able to reproduce their stickiness for good. The result? Velcro. **WIN!**

TODAY WAS:

❑ Okay ❑ Lame
❑ Good ❑ Bad
❑ Awesome ❑ Super crappy _____
❑ Epic ❑ Worst. Day. Ever. DATE

👎 TODAY'S FAIL:

❑ Average ❑ EPIC ❑ Super Mega EPIC ❑ So EPIC it's a WIN

❑ I / ❑ Who?_____ **DID WHAT?**_____

_____

_____

WHY? ❑ Totally meant to do that ❑ Drunk
❑ Trying to impress someone ❑ Just a jackass
❑ Other_____

WILL THE LOSERS INVOLVED HAVE TO:

❑ Go to the hospital? ❑ Move to a new town? ❑ Get plastic surgery?
❑ Get therapy? ❑ Other_____

LESSON LEARNED: _____

_____

❑ NEVER again ❑ Maybe again ❑ Do again at first opportunity

👍 TODODAY'S WIN:

☐ Above Average ☐ Massive ☐ EPIC ☐ Super Mega EPIC

☐ I / ☐ Who?_____ **DID WHAT?**_____

_____

_____

WHY? ☐ Totally awesome ☐ Preparation
☐ Deserved it ☐ Dumb luck
☐ Other_____

DID THE WIN RESULT IN A:

☐ New nickname? ☐ Hookup? ☐ Trophy?
☐ Arrest? ☐ Other_____

ALL HAIL_____, **RULER OF**_____!
(winner's name) (today's win)

> "Success is the ability to go from one failure to another with no loss of enthusiasm."
>
> **—WINSTON CHURCHILL**

TODAY WAS:

❏ Okay   ❏ Lame
❏ Good   ❏ Bad
❏ Awesome   ❏ Super crappy   _____
❏ Epic   ❏ Worst. Day. Ever.   DATE

👎 TODAY'S FAIL:

❏ Average   ❏ EPIC   ❏ Super Mega EPIC   ❏ So EPIC it's a WIN

❏ I / ❏ Who?_____ **DID WHAT?**_____

_____

_____

WHY? ❏ Totally meant to do that   ❏ Drunk
       ❏ Trying to impress someone   ❏ Just a jackass
       ❏ Other_____

WILL THE LOSERS INVOLVED HAVE TO:

❏ Go to the hospital?   ❏ Move to a new town?   ❏ Get plastic surgery?
❏ Get therapy?   ❏ Other_____

LESSON LEARNED: _____

_____

❏ NEVER again   ❏ Maybe again   ❏ Do again at first opportunity

👍 TODAY'S WIN:

☐ Above Average   ☐ Massive   ☐ EPIC   ☐ Super Mega EPIC

☐ I / ☐ Who?_____ **DID WHAT?**_____

_____

_____

WHY? ☐ Totally awesome   ☐ Preparation
          ☐ Deserved it   ☐ Dumb luck
          ☐ Other_____

DID THE WIN RESULT IN A:

☐ New nickname?   ☐ Hookup?   ☐ Trophy?
☐ Arrest?   ☐ Other_____

ALL HAIL_____, RULER OF_____!
            (winner's name)   (today's win)

FAIL⇨WIN: In 1943, a G.E. engineer named James Wright was
conducting an experiment with boric acid and silicone oil that resulted
in a useless blob of goo. Only it turned out not to be so useless after all.
He'd invented Silly Putty. **WIN!**

TODAY WAS:

- ❏ Okay
- ❏ Good
- ❏ Awesome
- ❏ Epic
- ❏ Lame
- ❏ Bad
- ❏ Super crappy
- ❏ Worst. Day. Ever.

DATE

👎 TODAY'S FAIL:

❏ Average ❏ EPIC ❏ Super Mega EPIC ❏ So EPIC it's a WIN

❏ I / ❏ Who?_____ **DID WHAT?**_____

_____

_____

WHY?
- ❏ Totally meant to do that
- ❏ Trying to impress someone
- ❏ Other_____
- ❏ Drunk
- ❏ Just a jackass

WILL THE LOSERS INVOLVED HAVE TO:

❏ Go to the hospital? ❏ Move to a new town? ❏ Get plastic surgery?
❏ Get therapy? ❏ Other_____

LESSON LEARNED:_____

_____

❏ NEVER again ❏ Maybe again ❏ Do again at first opportunity

👍 TODAY'S WIN:

☐ Above Average ☐ Massive ☐ EPIC ☐ Super Mega EPIC

☐ I / ☐ Who?_____ **DID WHAT?**_____

_____

WHY? ☐ Totally awesome ☐ Preparation
         ☐ Deserved it   ☐ Dumb luck
         ☐ Other_____

DID THE WIN RESULT IN A:

☐ New nickname? ☐ Hookup? ☐ Trophy?
☐ Arrest?   ☐ Other_____

ALL HAIL _____ **, RULER OF** _____ **!**
           (winner's name)   (today's win)

WIN/FAIL fact: The L to the forehead doesn't mean "loser" everywhere. In the Philippines, it's a political rallying gesture that means "Fight!" **WIN!**

TODAY WAS:

- ❑ Okay
- ❑ Good
- ❑ Awesome
- ❑ Epic
- ❑ Lame
- ❑ Bad
- ❑ Super crappy
- ❑ Worst. Day. Ever.

_____
DATE

👎 TODAY'S FAIL:

- ❑ Average
- ❑ EPIC
- ❑ Super Mega EPIC
- ❑ So EPIC it's a WIN

❑ I / ❑ Who?_____ **DID WHAT?**_____

_____

_____

WHY?
- ❑ Totally meant to do that
- ❑ Trying to impress someone
- ❑ Other_____
- ❑ Drunk
- ❑ Just a jackass

WILL THE LOSERS INVOLVED HAVE TO:

- ❑ Go to the hospital?
- ❑ Move to a new town?
- ❑ Get plastic surgery?
- ❑ Get therapy?
- ❑ Other_____

LESSON LEARNED: _____

_____

❑ NEVER again   ❑ Maybe again   ❑ Do again at first opportunity

👍 TODAY'S WIN:

☐ Above Average ☐ Massive ☐ EPIC ☐ Super Mega EPIC

☐ I / ☐ Who?_____ **DID WHAT?**_____

_____

_____

WHY? ☐ Totally awesome ☐ Preparation
☐ Deserved it ☐ Dumb luck
☐ Other_____

DID THE WIN RESULT IN A:

☐ New nickname? ☐ Hookup? ☐ Trophy?
☐ Arrest? ☐ Other_____

ALL HAIL _____ , RULER OF_____ !
(winner's name)   (today's win)

WIN/FAIL fact: The V for Victory sign does not mean "victory" everywhere.
In some countries, it means, "Up yours." **FAIL!**

TODAY WAS:

- ❏ Okay
- ❏ Good
- ❏ Awesome
- ❏ Epic
- ❏ Lame
- ❏ Bad
- ❏ Super crappy
- ❏ Worst. Day. Ever.

_____
DATE

👎 TODAY'S FAIL:

- ❏ Average
- ❏ EPIC
- ❏ Super Mega EPIC
- ❏ So EPIC it's a WIN

❏ I / ❏ Who?_____ **DID WHAT?**_____

_____

_____

WHY?
- ❏ Totally meant to do that
- ❏ Trying to impress someone
- ❏ Other_____
- ❏ Drunk
- ❏ Just a jackass

WILL THE LOSERS INVOLVED HAVE TO:

- ❏ Go to the hospital?
- ❏ Get therapy?
- ❏ Move to a new town?
- ❏ Other_____
- ❏ Get plastic surgery?

LESSON LEARNED:_____

_____

❏ NEVER again ❏ Maybe again ❏ Do again at first opportunity

👍 TODObuttonS'S WIN:

☐ Above Average   ☐ Massive   ☐ EPIC   ☐ Super Mega EPIC

☐ I / ☐ Who?_____ **DID WHAT?**_____

_____

_____

WHY? ☐ Totally awesome   ☐ Preparation
         ☐ Deserved it   ☐ Dumb luck
         ☐ Other_____

DID THE WIN RESULT IN A:

☐ New nickname?   ☐ Hookup?   ☐ Trophy?
☐ Arrest?   ☐ Other_____

ALL HAIL _____, RULER OF_____!
         (winner's name)   (today's win)

Schadenfreude is the German word for the feeling of pleasure we get
from another's misfortune, and it's what's behind our enjoyment of the
EPIC FAIL. There is no German word for pleasure in another's win.

TODAY WAS:

❏ Okay   ❏ Lame
❏ Good   ❏ Bad
❏ Awesome   ❏ Super crappy
❏ Epic   ❏ Worst. Day. Ever.

_____
DATE

👎 TODAY'S FAIL:

❏ Average   ❏ EPIC   ❏ Super Mega EPIC   ❏ So EPIC it's a WIN

❏ I / ❏ Who?_____ **DID WHAT?**_____

_____

_____

WHY?   ❏ Totally meant to do that   ❏ Drunk
       ❏ Trying to impress someone   ❏ Just a jackass
       ❏ Other_____

WILL THE LOSERS INVOLVED HAVE TO:

❏ Go to the hospital?   ❏ Move to a new town?   ❏ Get plastic surgery?
❏ Get therapy?   ❏ Other_____

LESSON LEARNED: _____

_____

❏ NEVER again   ❏ Maybe again   ❏ Do again at first opportunity

👍 TODEY'S WIN:

☐ Above Average   ☐ Massive   ☐ EPIC   ☐ Super Mega EPIC

☐ I / ☐ Who?_____ **DID WHAT?**_____

_____

_____

WHY? ☐ Totally awesome   ☐ Preparation
          ☐ Deserved it   ☐ Dumb luck
          ☐ Other_____

DID THE WIN RESULT IN A:

☐ New nickname?   ☐ Hookup?   ☐ Trophy?
☐ Arrest?   ☐ Other_____

ALL HAIL_____, RULER OF_____!
     (winner's name)   (today's win)

FAIL⇨WIN: In 1930, Ruth Wakefield was making a batch of chocolate cookies but didn't have time to melt and blend chocolate into the dough. So she threw in some chocolate chunks, figuring they'd melt into the dough in the oven. They didn't, and the chocolate chip cookie was born. **WIN!**

TODAY WAS:

❏ Okay ❏ Lame
❏ Good ❏ Bad
❏ Awesome ❏ Super crappy _____
❏ Epic ❏ Worst. Day. Ever. DATE

TODAY'S FAIL:

❏ Average ❏ EPIC ❏ Super Mega EPIC ❏ So EPIC it's a WIN

❏ I / ❏ Who?_____ **DID WHAT?**_____

_____

_____

WHY? ❏ Totally meant to do that ❏ Drunk
❏ Trying to impress someone ❏ Just a jackass
❏ Other_____

WILL THE LOSERS INVOLVED HAVE TO:

❏ Go to the hospital? ❏ Move to a new town? ❏ Get plastic surgery?
❏ Get therapy? ❏ Other_____

LESSON LEARNED:_____

_____

❏ NEVER again ❏ Maybe again ❏ Do again at first opportunity

👍 TODAY'S WIN:

❏ Above Average ❏ Massive ❏ EPIC ❏ Super Mega EPIC

❏ I / ❏ Who?_____ **DID WHAT?**_____

_____

_____

WHY? ❏ Totally awesome ❏ Preparation
          ❏ Deserved it   ❏ Dumb luck
          ❏ Other_____

DID THE WIN RESULT IN A:

❏ New nickname? ❏ Hookup? ❏ Trophy?
❏ Arrest?   ❏ Other_____

ALL HAIL_____, **RULER OF**_____!
        (winner's name)   (today's win)

If you're racking up a lot more **FAILs** than **WINs**, you may just need to
get more sleep. Being awake for twenty hours is equivalent to drinking
more than four beers. And a lot less fun.

TODAY WAS:

- ❏ Okay
- ❏ Good
- ❏ Awesome
- ❏ Epic
- ❏ Lame
- ❏ Bad
- ❏ Super crappy
- ❏ Worst. Day. Ever.

_____
DATE

👎 TODAY'S FAIL:

❏ Average ❏ EPIC ❏ Super Mega EPIC ❏ So EPIC it's a WIN

❏ I / ❏ Who?_____ **DID WHAT?**_____

_____

_____

WHY?
- ❏ Totally meant to do that
- ❏ Trying to impress someone
- ❏ Other_____
- ❏ Drunk
- ❏ Just a jackass

WILL THE LOSERS INVOLVED HAVE TO:

❏ Go to the hospital? ❏ Move to a new town? ❏ Get plastic surgery?
❏ Get therapy? ❏ Other_____

LESSON LEARNED: _____

_____

❏ NEVER again ❏ Maybe again ❏ Do again at first opportunity

👍 TODAY'S WIN: ◀

☐ Above Average   ☐ Massive   ☐ EPIC   ☐ Super Mega EPIC

☐ I / ☐ Who?_____ **DID WHAT?**_____

_____

_____

WHY? ☐ Totally awesome   ☐ Preparation
          ☐ Deserved it   ☐ Dumb luck
          ☐ Other_____

DID THE WIN RESULT IN A:

☐ New nickname?   ☐ Hookup?   ☐ Trophy?
☐ Arrest?   ☐ Other_____

ALL HAIL _____ , RULER OF_____ !
         (winner's name)   (today's win)

FAIL⇨WIN: Swiss engineer George de Mestral came home from a walk
and found a mess of burrs stuck to his clothes. He examined the burrs
under a microscope and thought he might be able to reproduce their
stickiness for good. The result? Velcro. **WIN!**

TODAY WAS:

- ❏ Okay
- ❏ Good
- ❏ Awesome
- ❏ Epic
- ❏ Lame
- ❏ Bad
- ❏ Super crappy
- ❏ Worst. Day. Ever.

_____
DATE

👎 TODAY'S FAIL:

- ❏ Average
- ❏ EPIC
- ❏ Super Mega EPIC
- ❏ So EPIC it's a WIN

❏ I / ❏ Who?_____ **DID WHAT?**_____

_____

_____

WHY?
- ❏ Totally meant to do that
- ❏ Trying to impress someone
- ❏ Other_____
- ❏ Drunk
- ❏ Just a jackass

WILL THE LOSERS INVOLVED HAVE TO:

- ❏ Go to the hospital?
- ❏ Get therapy?
- ❏ Move to a new town?
- ❏ Other_____
- ❏ Get plastic surgery?

LESSON LEARNED: _____

_____

❏ NEVER again ❏ Maybe again ❏ Do again at first opportunity

👍 TODAY'S WIN:

☐ Above Average ☐ Massive ☐ EPIC ☐ Super Mega EPIC

☐ I / ☐ Who?_____ **DID WHAT?**_____

_____

_____

WHY? ☐ Totally awesome ☐ Preparation
☐ Deserved it ☐ Dumb luck
☐ Other_____

DID THE WIN RESULT IN A:

☐ New nickname? ☐ Hookup? ☐ Trophy?
☐ Arrest? ☐ Other_____

ALL HAIL_____, RULER OF_____!
(winner's name) (today's win)

"Success is the ability to go from one failure to another with no loss of enthusiasm."

—WINSTON CHURCHILL

TODAY WAS:

- ❑ Okay
- ❑ Good
- ❑ Awesome
- ❑ Epic
- ❑ Lame
- ❑ Bad
- ❑ Super crappy
- ❑ Worst. Day. Ever.

_____

DATE

👎 TODAY'S FAIL:

- ❑ Average
- ❑ EPIC
- ❑ Super Mega EPIC
- ❑ So EPIC it's a WIN

❑ I / ❑ Who?_____ **DID WHAT?**_____

_____

_____

WHY?
- ❑ Totally meant to do that
- ❑ Trying to impress someone
- ❑ Other_____
- ❑ Drunk
- ❑ Just a jackass

WILL THE LOSERS INVOLVED HAVE TO:

- ❑ Go to the hospital?
- ❑ Get therapy?
- ❑ Move to a new town?
- ❑ Other_____
- ❑ Get plastic surgery?

LESSON LEARNED: _____

_____

❑ NEVER again ❑ Maybe again ❑ Do again at first opportunity

👍 TODAY'S WIN:

❏ Above Average   ❏ Massive   ❏ EPIC   ❏ Super Mega EPIC

❏ I / ❏ Who?_____ **DID WHAT?**_____

_____

_____

WHY? ❏ Totally awesome   ❏ Preparation
          ❏ Deserved it   ❏ Dumb luck
          ❏ Other_____

DID THE WIN RESULT IN A:

❏ New nickname?   ❏ Hookup?   ❏ Trophy?
❏ Arrest?   ❏ Other_____

ALL HAIL _____ , RULER OF_____ !
         (winner's name)   (today's win)

FAIL⇨WIN: In 1943, a G.E. engineer named James Wright was conducting an experiment with boric acid and silicone oil that resulted in a useless blob of goo. Only it turned out not to be so useless after all. He'd invented Silly Putty. **WIN!**

TODAY WAS:

- ❏ Okay
- ❏ Good
- ❏ Awesome
- ❏ Epic
- ❏ Lame
- ❏ Bad
- ❏ Super crappy
- ❏ Worst. Day. Ever.

_____
DATE

👎 TODAY'S FAIL:

❏ Average   ❏ EPIC   ❏ Super Mega EPIC   ❏ So EPIC it's a WIN

❏ I / ❏ Who?_____ **DID WHAT?**_____

_____

_____

WHY?
- ❏ Totally meant to do that
- ❏ Trying to impress someone
- ❏ Other_____
- ❏ Drunk
- ❏ Just a jackass

WILL THE LOSERS INVOLVED HAVE TO:

❏ Go to the hospital?   ❏ Move to a new town?   ❏ Get plastic surgery?

❏ Get therapy?   ❏ Other_____

LESSON LEARNED: _____

_____

❏ NEVER again   ❏ Maybe again   ❏ Do again at first opportunity

👍 TODOS'S WIN:

☐ Above Average ☐ Massive ☐ EPIC ☐ Super Mega EPIC

☐ I / ☐ Who?_____ **DID WHAT?**_____

_____

_____

WHY? ☐ Totally awesome   ☐ Preparation
         ☐ Deserved it   ☐ Dumb luck
         ☐ Other_____

DID THE WIN RESULT IN A:

☐ New nickname?   ☐ Hookup?   ☐ Trophy?
☐ Arrest?   ☐ Other_____

ALL HAIL_____, **RULER OF**_____!
         (winner's name)   (today's win)

WIN/FAIL fact: The L to the forehead doesn't mean "loser" everywhere. In the Philippines, it's a political rallying gesture that means "Fight!" **WIN!**

TODAY WAS:

- ❏ Okay
- ❏ Good
- ❏ Awesome
- ❏ Epic
- ❏ Lame
- ❏ Bad
- ❏ Super crappy
- ❏ Worst. Day. Ever.

_____
DATE

👎 TODAY'S FAIL:

- ❏ Average
- ❏ EPIC
- ❏ Super Mega EPIC
- ❏ So EPIC it's a WIN

❏ I / ❏ Who?_____ **DID WHAT?**_____

_____

_____

WHY?
- ❏ Totally meant to do that
- ❏ Trying to impress someone
- ❏ Other_____
- ❏ Drunk
- ❏ Just a jackass

WILL THE LOSERS INVOLVED HAVE TO:

- ❏ Go to the hospital?
- ❏ Get therapy?
- ❏ Move to a new town?
- ❏ Other_____
- ❏ Get plastic surgery?

LESSON LEARNED: _____

_____

❏ NEVER again   ❏ Maybe again   ❏ Do again at first opportunity

👍 TODODAY'S WIN:

☐ Above Average   ☐ Massive   ☐ EPIC   ☐ Super Mega EPIC

☐ I / ☐ Who?_____ **DID WHAT?**_____

_____

_____

WHY?   ☐ Totally awesome   ☐ Preparation
      ☐ Deserved it   ☐ Dumb luck
      ☐ Other_____

DID THE WIN RESULT IN A:

☐ New nickname?   ☐ Hookup?   ☐ Trophy?
☐ Arrest?   ☐ Other_____

ALL HAIL _____ , RULER OF_____!
        (winner's name)   (today's win)

WIN/FAIL fact: The V for Victory sign does not mean "victory" everywhere. In some countries, it means, "Up yours." **FAIL!**

TODAY WAS:
- ❏ Okay
- ❏ Good
- ❏ Awesome
- ❏ Epic
- ❏ Lame
- ❏ Bad
- ❏ Super crappy
- ❏ Worst. Day. Ever.

_____ DATE

👎 TODAY'S FAIL:

- ❏ Average
- ❏ EPIC
- ❏ Super Mega EPIC
- ❏ So EPIC it's a WIN

❏ I / ❏ Who?_____ **DID WHAT?**_____

_____

_____

WHY?
- ❏ Totally meant to do that
- ❏ Trying to impress someone
- ❏ Other_____
- ❏ Drunk
- ❏ Just a jackass

WILL THE LOSERS INVOLVED HAVE TO:

❏ Go to the hospital? ❏ Move to a new town? ❏ Get plastic surgery?
❏ Get therapy? ❏ Other_____

LESSON LEARNED: _____

_____

❏ NEVER again ❏ Maybe again ❏ Do again at first opportunity

👍 TODAY'S WIN:

□ Above Average □ Massive □ EPIC □ Super Mega EPIC

□ I / □ Who?_____ **DID WHAT?**_____

_____

_____

WHY? □ Totally awesome   □ Preparation
        □ Deserved it   □ Dumb luck
        □ Other_____

DID THE WIN RESULT IN A:

□ New nickname?   □ Hookup?   □ Trophy?
□ Arrest?   □ Other_____

ALL HAIL _____, RULER OF_____!
        (winner's name)   (today's win)

Schadenfreude is the German word for the feeling of pleasure we get
from another's misfortune, and it's what's behind our enjoyment of the
EPIC FAIL. There is no German word for pleasure in another's win.

TODAY WAS:

- ❑ Okay
- ❑ Good
- ❑ Awesome
- ❑ Epic
- ❑ Lame
- ❑ Bad
- ❑ Super crappy
- ❑ Worst. Day. Ever.

_____ DATE

👎 TODAY'S FAIL:

- ❑ Average
- ❑ EPIC
- ❑ Super Mega EPIC
- ❑ So EPIC it's a WIN

❑ I / ❑ Who?_____ **DID WHAT?**_____

_____

_____

WHY?
- ❑ Totally meant to do that
- ❑ Trying to impress someone
- ❑ Other_____
- ❑ Drunk
- ❑ Just a jackass

WILL THE LOSERS INVOLVED HAVE TO:

- ❑ Go to the hospital? ❑ Move to a new town? ❑ Get plastic surgery?
- ❑ Get therapy? ❑ Other_____

LESSON LEARNED:_____

_____

❑ NEVER again ❑ Maybe again ❑ Do again at first opportunity

👍 TODODAY'S WIN: ◀

□ Above Average   □ Massive   □ EPIC   □ Super Mega EPIC

□ I / □ Who?_____ **DID WHAT?**_____

_____

_____

WHY? □ Totally awesome   □ Preparation
          □ Deserved it   □ Dumb luck
          □ Other_____

DID THE WIN RESULT IN A:

□ New nickname?   □ Hookup?   □ Trophy?
□ Arrest?   □ Other_____

ALL HAIL _____, **RULER OF**_____!
              (winner's name)   (today's win)

FAIL⇨WIN: In 1930, Ruth Wakefield was making a batch of chocolate cookies but didn't have time to melt and blend chocolate into the dough. So she threw in some chocolate chunks, figuring they'd melt into the dough in the oven. They didn't, and the chocolate chip cookie was born. **WIN!**

TODAY WAS:

- ❏ Okay
- ❏ Good
- ❏ Awesome
- ❏ Epic
- ❏ Lame
- ❏ Bad
- ❏ Super crappy
- ❏ Worst. Day. Ever.

_____

DATE

👎 TODAY'S FAIL:

- ❏ Average
- ❏ EPIC
- ❏ Super Mega EPIC
- ❏ So EPIC it's a WIN

❏ I / ❏ Who?_____ **DID WHAT?**_____

_____

_____

WHY?
- ❏ Totally meant to do that
- ❏ Trying to impress someone
- ❏ Other_____
- ❏ Drunk
- ❏ Just a jackass

WILL THE LOSERS INVOLVED HAVE TO:

- ❏ Go to the hospital?
- ❏ Move to a new town?
- ❏ Get plastic surgery?
- ❏ Get therapy?
- ❏ Other_____

LESSON LEARNED:_____

_____

❏ NEVER again ❏ Maybe again ❏ Do again at first opportunity

👍 TODAY'S WIN:

❏ Above Average   ❏ Massive   ❏ EPIC   ❏ Super Mega EPIC

❏ I / ❏ Who?_____ **DID WHAT?**_____

_____

_____

WHY? ❏ Totally awesome   ❏ Preparation
         ❏ Deserved it   ❏ Dumb luck
         ❏ Other_____

DID THE WIN RESULT IN A:

❏ New nickname?   ❏ Hookup?   ❏ Trophy?
❏ Arrest?   ❏ Other_____

ALL HAIL _____ , RULER OF _____ !
         (winner's name)   (today's win)

If you're racking up a lot more **FAILs** than **WINs**, you may just need to get more sleep. Being awake for twenty hours is equivalent to drinking more than four beers. And a lot less fun.

TODAY WAS:

- ❏ Okay
- ❏ Good
- ❏ Awesome
- ❏ Epic
- ❏ Lame
- ❏ Bad
- ❏ Super crappy
- ❏ Worst. Day. Ever.

_____
DATE

👎 TODAY'S FAIL:

- ❏ Average
- ❏ EPIC
- ❏ Super Mega EPIC
- ❏ So EPIC it's a WIN

❏ I / ❏ Who?_____ **DID WHAT?**_____

_____

_____

WHY?
- ❏ Totally meant to do that
- ❏ Trying to impress someone
- ❏ Other_____
- ❏ Drunk
- ❏ Just a jackass

WILL THE LOSERS INVOLVED HAVE TO:

- ❏ Go to the hospital?
- ❏ Get therapy?
- ❏ Move to a new town?
- ❏ Other_____
- ❏ Get plastic surgery?

LESSON LEARNED: _____

_____

❏ NEVER again   ❏ Maybe again   ❏ Do again at first opportunity

👍 TODODAY'S WIN:

☐ Above Average   ☐ Massive   ☐ EPIC   ☐ Super Mega EPIC

☐ I / ☐ Who?_____ **DID WHAT?**_____

_____

_____

WHY? ☐ Totally awesome   ☐ Preparation
          ☐ Deserved it   ☐ Dumb luck
          ☐ Other_____

DID THE WIN RESULT IN A:

☐ New nickname?   ☐ Hookup?   ☐ Trophy?
☐ Arrest?   ☐ Other_____

ALL HAIL _____ , **RULER OF**_____ !
             (winner's name)   (today's win)

FAIL⇨WIN: Swiss engineer George de Mestral came home from a walk and found a mess of burrs stuck to his clothes. He examined the burrs under a microscope and thought he might be able to reproduce their stickiness for good. The result? Velcro. **WIN!**

TODAY WAS:

❑ Okay   ❑ Lame
❑ Good   ❑ Bad
❑ Awesome   ❑ Super crappy   DATE _____
❑ Epic   ❑ Worst. Day. Ever.

👎 TODAY'S FAIL:

❑ Average   ❑ EPIC   ❑ Super Mega EPIC   ❑ So EPIC it's a WIN

❑ I / ❑ Who?_____ **DID WHAT?** _____

_____

_____

WHY? ❑ Totally meant to do that   ❑ Drunk
        ❑ Trying to impress someone   ❑ Just a jackass
        ❑ Other_____

WILL THE LOSERS INVOLVED HAVE TO:

❑ Go to the hospital?   ❑ Move to a new town?   ❑ Get plastic surgery?
❑ Get therapy?   ❑ Other_____

LESSON LEARNED: _____

_____

❑ NEVER again   ❑ Maybe again   ❑ Do again at first opportunity

👍 TODAY'S WIN:

□ Above Average   □ Massive   □ EPIC   □ Super Mega EPIC

□ I / □ Who?_____ **DID WHAT?**_____

_____

_____

WHY?   □ Totally awesome   □ Preparation
        □ Deserved it   □ Dumb luck
        □ Other_____

DID THE WIN RESULT IN A:

□ New nickname?   □ Hookup?   □ Trophy?
□ Arrest?   □ Other_____

ALL HAIL _____ **, RULER OF** _____ **!**
          (winner's name)   (today's win)

> *"Success is the ability to go from one failure to another with no loss of enthusiasm."*
>
> **—WINSTON CHURCHILL**

TODAY WAS:

❏ Okay ❏ Lame
❏ Good ❏ Bad
❏ Awesome ❏ Super crappy
❏ Epic ❏ Worst. Day. Ever.

_____
DATE

👎 TODAY'S FAIL:

❏ Average ❏ EPIC ❏ Super Mega EPIC ❏ So EPIC it's a WIN

❏ I / ❏ Who?_____ **DID WHAT?**_____

_____

_____

WHY? ❏ Totally meant to do that ❏ Drunk
❏ Trying to impress someone ❏ Just a jackass
❏ Other_____

WILL THE LOSERS INVOLVED HAVE TO:

❏ Go to the hospital? ❏ Move to a new town? ❏ Get plastic surgery?
❏ Get therapy? ❏ Other_____

LESSON LEARNED:_____

_____

❏ NEVER again ❏ Maybe again ❏ Do again at first opportunity

👍 TODAY'S WIN:

☐ Above Average   ☐ Massive   ☐ EPIC   ☐ Super Mega EPIC

☐ I / ☐ Who?_____ **DID WHAT?**_____

_____

_____

WHY?   ☐ Totally awesome   ☐ Preparation
       ☐ Deserved it   ☐ Dumb luck
       ☐ Other_____

DID THE WIN RESULT IN A:

☐ New nickname?   ☐ Hookup?   ☐ Trophy?
☐ Arrest?   ☐ Other_____

ALL HAIL _____, RULER OF_____!
           (winner's name)   (today's win)

FAIL⇨WIN: In 1943, a G.E. engineer named James Wright was conducting an experiment with boric acid and silicone oil that resulted in a useless blob of goo. Only it turned out not to be so useless after all. He'd invented Silly Putty. **WIN!**

TODAY WAS:

- ❑ Okay
- ❑ Good
- ❑ Awesome
- ❑ Epic
- ❑ Lame
- ❑ Bad
- ❑ Super crappy
- ❑ Worst. Day. Ever.

_____
DATE

👎 TODAY'S FAIL:

- ❑ Average
- ❑ EPIC
- ❑ Super Mega EPIC
- ❑ So EPIC it's a WIN

❑ I / ❑ Who?_____ **DID WHAT?**_____

_____

_____

WHY?
- ❑ Totally meant to do that
- ❑ Trying to impress someone
- ❑ Other_____
- ❑ Drunk
- ❑ Just a jackass

WILL THE LOSERS INVOLVED HAVE TO:

❑ Go to the hospital? ❑ Move to a new town? ❑ Get plastic surgery?
❑ Get therapy? ❑ Other_____

LESSON LEARNED: _____

_____

❑ NEVER again ❑ Maybe again ❑ Do again at first opportunity

👍 TODAY'S WIN:

☐ Above Average   ☐ Massive   ☐ EPIC   ☐ Super Mega EPIC

☐ I / ☐ Who?_____ **DID WHAT?**_____

_____

_____

WHY?   ☐ Totally awesome   ☐ Preparation
          ☐ Deserved it   ☐ Dumb luck
          ☐ Other_____

DID THE WIN RESULT IN A:

☐ New nickname?   ☐ Hookup?   ☐ Trophy?
☐ Arrest?   ☐ Other_____

ALL HAIL_____**, RULER OF**_____**!**
         (winner's name)   (today's win)

WIN/FAIL fact: The L to the forehead doesn't mean "loser" everywhere. In the Philippines, it's a political rallying gesture that means "Fight!" **WIN!**

TODAY WAS:

- ❏ Okay
- ❏ Good
- ❏ Awesome
- ❏ Epic
- ❏ Lame
- ❏ Bad
- ❏ Super crappy
- ❏ Worst. Day. Ever.

_____
DATE

👎 TODAY'S FAIL:

- ❏ Average
- ❏ EPIC
- ❏ Super Mega EPIC
- ❏ So EPIC it's a WIN

❏ I / ❏ Who?_____ **DID WHAT?**_____

_____

_____

WHY?
- ❏ Totally meant to do that
- ❏ Trying to impress someone
- ❏ Other_____
- ❏ Drunk
- ❏ Just a jackass

WILL THE LOSERS INVOLVED HAVE TO:

- ❏ Go to the hospital?
- ❏ Get therapy?
- ❏ Move to a new town?
- ❏ Other_____
- ❏ Get plastic surgery?

LESSON LEARNED: _____

_____

❏ NEVER again ❏ Maybe again ❏ Do again at first opportunity

👍 TODODAY'S WIN:

☐ Above Average   ☐ Massive   ☐ EPIC   ☐ Super Mega EPIC

☐ I / ☐ Who?_____ **DID WHAT?**_____

_____

_____

WHY?
☐ Totally awesome   ☐ Preparation
☐ Deserved it   ☐ Dumb luck
☐ Other_____

DID THE WIN RESULT IN A:

☐ New nickname?   ☐ Hookup?   ☐ Trophy?
☐ Arrest?   ☐ Other_____

ALL HAIL_____, **RULER OF**_____!
   (winner's name)   (today's win)

WIN/FAIL fact: The V for Victory sign does not mean "victory" everywhere. In some countries, it means, "Up yours." **FAIL!**

TODAY WAS:

- ❑ Okay
- ❑ Good
- ❑ Awesome
- ❑ Epic
- ❑ Lame
- ❑ Bad
- ❑ Super crappy
- ❑ Worst. Day. Ever.

_____
DATE

👎 TODAY'S FAIL:

- ❑ Average
- ❑ EPIC
- ❑ Super Mega EPIC
- ❑ So EPIC it's a WIN

❑ I / ❑ Who?_____ **DID WHAT?**_____

_____

_____

WHY?
- ❑ Totally meant to do that
- ❑ Trying to impress someone
- ❑ Other_____
- ❑ Drunk
- ❑ Just a jackass

WILL THE LOSERS INVOLVED HAVE TO:

- ❑ Go to the hospital?
- ❑ Get therapy?
- ❑ Move to a new town?
- ❑ Other_____
- ❑ Get plastic surgery?

LESSON LEARNED:_____

_____

❑ NEVER again ❑ Maybe again ❑ Do again at first opportunity

👍 TODAY'S WIN:

☐ Above Average   ☐ Massive   ☐ EPIC   ☐ Super Mega EPIC

☐ I / ☐ Who?_____ **DID WHAT?**_____

_____

_____

WHY?   ☐ Totally awesome   ☐ Preparation
          ☐ Deserved it   ☐ Dumb luck
          ☐ Other_____

DID THE WIN RESULT IN A:

☐ New nickname?   ☐ Hookup?   ☐ Trophy?
☐ Arrest?   ☐ Other_____

ALL HAIL _____ , RULER OF _____ !
         (winner's name)   (today's win)

Schadenfreude is the German word for the feeling of pleasure we get
from another's misfortune, and it's what's behind our enjoyment of the
EPIC FAIL. There is no German word for pleasure in another's win.

TODAY WAS:

- ❏ Okay
- ❏ Good
- ❏ Awesome
- ❏ Epic
- ❏ Lame
- ❏ Bad
- ❏ Super crappy
- ❏ Worst. Day. Ever.

_____
DATE

👎 TODAY'S FAIL:

- ❏ Average
- ❏ EPIC
- ❏ Super Mega EPIC
- ❏ So EPIC it's a WIN

❏ I / ❏ Who?_____ **DID WHAT?**_____

_____

_____

WHY?
- ❏ Totally meant to do that
- ❏ Trying to impress someone
- ❏ Other_____
- ❏ Drunk
- ❏ Just a jackass

WILL THE LOSERS INVOLVED HAVE TO:

- ❏ Go to the hospital?
- ❏ Get therapy?
- ❏ Move to a new town?
- ❏ Other_____
- ❏ Get plastic surgery?

LESSON LEARNED:_____

_____

❏ NEVER again ❏ Maybe again ❏ Do again at first opportunity

👍 TODAY'S WIN:

☐ Above Average   ☐ Massive   ☐ EPIC   ☐ Super Mega EPIC

☐ I / ☐ Who?_____ **DID WHAT?**_____

_____

_____

WHY?
☐ Totally awesome   ☐ Preparation
☐ Deserved it   ☐ Dumb luck
☐ Other_____

DID THE WIN RESULT IN A:

☐ New nickname?   ☐ Hookup?   ☐ Trophy?
☐ Arrest?   ☐ Other_____

ALL HAIL _____, RULER OF_____ !
(winner's name)   (today's win)

FAIL⇨WIN: In 1930, Ruth Wakefield was making a batch of chocolate cookies but didn't have time to melt and blend chocolate into the dough. So she threw in some chocolate chunks, figuring they'd melt into the dough in the oven. They didn't, and the chocolate chip cookie was born. **WIN!**

TODAY WAS:

- ❑ Okay
- ❑ Good
- ❑ Awesome
- ❑ Epic
- ❑ Lame
- ❑ Bad
- ❑ Super crappy
- ❑ Worst. Day. Ever.

_____
DATE

👎 TODAY'S FAIL:

- ❑ Average
- ❑ EPIC
- ❑ Super Mega EPIC
- ❑ So EPIC it's a WIN

❑ I / ❑ Who?_____ **DID WHAT?**_____

_____

_____

WHY?
- ❑ Totally meant to do that
- ❑ Trying to impress someone
- ❑ Other_____
- ❑ Drunk
- ❑ Just a jackass

WILL THE LOSERS INVOLVED HAVE TO:

- ❑ Go to the hospital?
- ❑ Get therapy?
- ❑ Move to a new town?
- ❑ Other_____
- ❑ Get plastic surgery?

LESSON LEARNED: _____

_____

❑ NEVER again   ❑ Maybe again   ❑ Do again at first opportunity

👍 TODODAY'S WIN:

☐ Above Average   ☐ Massive   ☐ EPIC   ☐ Super Mega EPIC

☐ I / ☐ Who?_____ **DID WHAT?**_____

_____

_____

WHY?   ☐ Totally awesome   ☐ Preparation
       ☐ Deserved it   ☐ Dumb luck
       ☐ Other_____

DID THE WIN RESULT IN A:

☐ New nickname?   ☐ Hookup?   ☐ Trophy?
☐ Arrest?   ☐ Other_____

ALL HAIL _____ , RULER OF_____ !
        (winner's name)   (today's win)

If you're racking up a lot more **FAILs** than **WINs**, you may just need to get more sleep. Being awake for twenty hours is equivalent to drinking more than four beers. And a lot less fun.

TODAY WAS:

- ❏ Okay
- ❏ Good
- ❏ Awesome
- ❏ Epic
- ❏ Lame
- ❏ Bad
- ❏ Super crappy
- ❏ Worst. Day. Ever.

_____
DATE

👎 **TODAY'S FAIL:**

❏ Average ❏ EPIC ❏ Super Mega EPIC ❏ So EPIC it's a WIN

❏ I / ❏ Who?_____ **DID WHAT?**_____

_____

_____

WHY?
- ❏ Totally meant to do that
- ❏ Trying to impress someone
- ❏ Other_____
- ❏ Drunk
- ❏ Just a jackass

WILL THE LOSERS INVOLVED HAVE TO:

❏ Go to the hospital? ❏ Move to a new town? ❏ Get plastic surgery?
❏ Get therapy? ❏ Other_____

LESSON LEARNED:_____

_____

❏ NEVER again ❏ Maybe again ❏ Do again at first opportunity

👍 TODODAY'S WIN:

- ☐ Above Average   ☐ Massive   ☐ EPIC   ☐ Super Mega EPIC

☐ I / ☐ Who?_____ **DID WHAT?**_____

_____

_____

WHY?
- ☐ Totally awesome   ☐ Preparation
- ☐ Deserved it   ☐ Dumb luck
- ☐ Other_____

DID THE WIN RESULT IN A:

- ☐ New nickname?   ☐ Hookup?   ☐ Trophy?
- ☐ Arrest?   ☐ Other_____

ALL HAIL_____, RULER OF_____!
(winner's name)   (today's win)

FAIL⇨WIN: Swiss engineer George de Mestral came home from a walk and found a mess of burrs stuck to his clothes. He examined the burrs under a microscope and thought he might be able to reproduce their stickiness for good. The result? Velcro. **WIN!**

TODAY WAS:

- ❑ Okay
- ❑ Good
- ❑ Awesome
- ❑ Epic
- ❑ Lame
- ❑ Bad
- ❑ Super crappy
- ❑ Worst. Day. Ever.

_____

DATE

👎 TODAY'S FAIL:

- ❑ Average
- ❑ EPIC
- ❑ Super Mega EPIC
- ❑ So EPIC it's a WIN

❑ I / ❑ Who?_____ **DID WHAT?**_____

_____

_____

WHY?
- ❑ Totally meant to do that
- ❑ Trying to impress someone
- ❑ Other_____
- ❑ Drunk
- ❑ Just a jackass

WILL THE LOSERS INVOLVED HAVE TO:

- ❑ Go to the hospital?
- ❑ Move to a new town?
- ❑ Get plastic surgery?
- ❑ Get therapy?
- ❑ Other_____

LESSON LEARNED: _____

_____

❑ NEVER again   ❑ Maybe again   ❑ Do again at first opportunity

👍 TODANK TODAY'S WIN:

☐ Above Average ☐ Massive ☐ EPIC ☐ Super Mega EPIC

☐ I / ☐ Who?_____ **DID WHAT?**_____

_____

_____

WHY? ☐ Totally awesome ☐ Preparation
☐ Deserved it ☐ Dumb luck
☐ Other_____

DID THE WIN RESULT IN A:

☐ New nickname? ☐ Hookup? ☐ Trophy?
☐ Arrest? ☐ Other_____

ALL HAIL _____, RULER OF_____!
(winner's name)   (today's win)

> "Success is the ability to go from one failure to another with no loss of enthusiasm."
>
> **—WINSTON CHURCHILL**

TODAY WAS:

- ❏ Okay
- ❏ Good
- ❏ Awesome
- ❏ Epic
- ❏ Lame
- ❏ Bad
- ❏ Super crappy
- ❏ Worst. Day. Ever.

_____
DATE

👎 TODAY'S FAIL:

- ❏ Average
- ❏ EPIC
- ❏ Super Mega EPIC
- ❏ So EPIC it's a WIN

❏ I / ❏ Who?_____ **DID WHAT?**_____

_____

_____

WHY?
- ❏ Totally meant to do that
- ❏ Trying to impress someone
- ❏ Other_____
- ❏ Drunk
- ❏ Just a jackass

WILL THE LOSERS INVOLVED HAVE TO:

- ❏ Go to the hospital?
- ❏ Get therapy?
- ❏ Move to a new town?
- ❏ Other_____
- ❏ Get plastic surgery?

LESSON LEARNED: _____

_____

❏ NEVER again ❏ Maybe again ❏ Do again at first opportunity

👍 TODAY'S WIN:

☐ Above Average   ☐ Massive   ☐ EPIC   ☐ Super Mega EPIC

☐ I / ☐ Who?_____ **DID WHAT?**_____

_____

_____

WHY?   ☐ Totally awesome   ☐ Preparation
           ☐ Deserved it   ☐ Dumb luck
           ☐ Other_____

DID THE WIN RESULT IN A:

☐ New nickname?   ☐ Hookup?   ☐ Trophy?
☐ Arrest?   ☐ Other_____

ALL HAIL _____ , RULER OF _____ !
     (winner's name)   (today's win)

FAIL⇨WIN: In 1943, a G.E. engineer named James Wright was conducting an experiment with boric acid and silicone oil that resulted in a useless blob of goo. Only it turned out not to be so useless after all. He'd invented Silly Putty. **WIN!**

TODAY WAS:

- ❑ Okay
- ❑ Good
- ❑ Awesome
- ❑ Epic
- ❑ Lame
- ❑ Bad
- ❑ Super crappy
- ❑ Worst. Day. Ever.

_____
DATE

👎 TODAY'S FAIL:

- ❑ Average ❑ EPIC ❑ Super Mega EPIC ❑ So EPIC it's a WIN

❑ I / ❑ Who?_____ **DID WHAT?**_____

_____

_____

WHY?

- ❑ Totally meant to do that
- ❑ Trying to impress someone
- ❑ Other_____
- ❑ Drunk
- ❑ Just a jackass

WILL THE LOSERS INVOLVED HAVE TO:

- ❑ Go to the hospital? ❑ Move to a new town? ❑ Get plastic surgery?
- ❑ Get therapy? ❑ Other_____

LESSON LEARNED: _____

_____

❑ NEVER again ❑ Maybe again ❑ Do again at first opportunity

👍 TODStay'S WIN: ◀

☐ Above Average   ☐ Massive   ☐ EPIC   ☐ Super Mega EPIC

☐ I / ☐ Who?_____ **DID WHAT?**_____

_____

_____

WHY?   ☐ Totally awesome   ☐ Preparation
          ☐ Deserved it   ☐ Dumb luck
          ☐ Other_____

DID THE WIN RESULT IN A:

☐ New nickname?   ☐ Hookup?   ☐ Trophy?
☐ Arrest?   ☐ Other_____

ALL HAIL _____ , RULER OF_____ !
(winner's name)   (today's win)

WIN/FAIL fact: The L to the forehead doesn't mean "loser" everywhere. In the Philippines, it's a political rallying gesture that means "Fight!" **WIN!**

TODAY WAS:

❏ Okay   ❏ Lame
❏ Good   ❏ Bad
❏ Awesome   ❏ Super crappy   **DATE**
❏ Epic   ❏ Worst. Day. Ever.

👎 TODAY'S FAIL:

❏ Average   ❏ EPIC   ❏ Super Mega EPIC   ❏ So EPIC it's a WIN

❏ I / ❏ Who?_____ **DID WHAT?**_____

_____

_____

WHY?
❏ Totally meant to do that   ❏ Drunk
❏ Trying to impress someone   ❏ Just a jackass
❏ Other_____

WILL THE LOSERS INVOLVED HAVE TO:

❏ Go to the hospital?   ❏ Move to a new town?   ❏ Get plastic surgery?
❏ Get therapy?   ❏ Other_____

LESSON LEARNED:_____

_____

❏ NEVER again   ❏ Maybe again   ❏ Do again at first opportunity

👍 TODODAY'S WIN:

☐ Above Average   ☐ Massive   ☐ EPIC   ☐ Super Mega EPIC

☐ I / ☐ Who?_____ **DID WHAT?**_____

_____

_____

WHY? ☐ Totally awesome   ☐ Preparation
         ☐ Deserved it   ☐ Dumb luck
         ☐ Other_____

DID THE WIN RESULT IN A:

☐ New nickname?   ☐ Hookup?   ☐ Trophy?
☐ Arrest?   ☐ Other_____

ALL HAIL _____, RULER OF _____!
        (winner's name)   (today's win)

WIN/FAIL fact: The V for Victory sign does not mean "victory" everywhere.
In some countries, it means, "Up yours." **FAIL!**

TODAY WAS:

- ❑ Okay
- ❑ Good
- ❑ Awesome
- ❑ Epic
- ❑ Lame
- ❑ Bad
- ❑ Super crappy
- ❑ Worst. Day. Ever.

_____
DATE

👎 TODAY'S FAIL:

- ❑ Average
- ❑ EPIC
- ❑ Super Mega EPIC
- ❑ So EPIC it's a WIN

❑ I / ❑ Who?_____ **DID WHAT?**_____

_____

_____

WHY?
- ❑ Totally meant to do that
- ❑ Trying to impress someone
- ❑ Other_____
- ❑ Drunk
- ❑ Just a jackass

WILL THE LOSERS INVOLVED HAVE TO:

- ❑ Go to the hospital?
- ❑ Get therapy?
- ❑ Move to a new town?
- ❑ Other_____
- ❑ Get plastic surgery?

LESSON LEARNED:_____

_____

❑ NEVER again   ❑ Maybe again   ❑ Do again at first opportunity

👍 TODAY'S WIN:

❏ Above Average   ❏ Massive   ❏ EPIC   ❏ Super Mega EPIC

❏ I / ❏ Who?_____ **DID WHAT?**_____

_____

_____

WHY? ❏ Totally awesome   ❏ Preparation
        ❏ Deserved it   ❏ Dumb luck
        ❏ Other_____

DID THE WIN RESULT IN A:

❏ New nickname?   ❏ Hookup?   ❏ Trophy?
❏ Arrest?   ❏ Other_____

ALL HAIL _____ , RULER OF _____ !
            (winner's name)   (today's win)

Schadenfreude is the German word for the feeling of pleasure we get from another's misfortune, and it's what's behind our enjoyment of the **EPIC FAIL.** There is no German word for pleasure in another's win.

TODAY WAS:

- ❏ Okay
- ❏ Good
- ❏ Awesome
- ❏ Epic
- ❏ Lame
- ❏ Bad
- ❏ Super crappy
- ❏ Worst. Day. Ever.

_____ DATE

👎 TODAY'S FAIL:

- ❏ Average
- ❏ EPIC
- ❏ Super Mega EPIC
- ❏ So EPIC it's a WIN

❏ I / ❏ Who?_____ **DID WHAT?**_____

_____

_____

WHY?
- ❏ Totally meant to do that
- ❏ Trying to impress someone
- ❏ Other_____
- ❏ Drunk
- ❏ Just a jackass

WILL THE LOSERS INVOLVED HAVE TO:

- ❏ Go to the hospital?
- ❏ Get therapy?
- ❏ Move to a new town?
- ❏ Other_____
- ❏ Get plastic surgery?

LESSON LEARNED:_____

_____

❏ NEVER again   ❏ Maybe again   ❏ Do again at first opportunity

👍 TODODAY'S WIN:

☐ Above Average　☐ Massive　☐ EPIC　☐ Super Mega EPIC

☐ I / ☐ Who?_____ **DID WHAT?**_____

_____

_____

WHY?　☐ Totally awesome　☐ Preparation
　　　　☐ Deserved it　　　☐ Dumb luck
　　　　☐ Other_____

DID THE WIN RESULT IN A:

☐ New nickname?　☐ Hookup?　☐ Trophy?
☐ Arrest?　　　　☐ Other_____

ALL HAIL_____, RULER OF_____!
　　　　　(winner's name)　　　　　　　　(today's win)

FAIL⇨WIN: In 1930, Ruth Wakefield was making a batch of chocolate cookies but didn't have time to melt and blend chocolate into the dough. So she threw in some chocolate chunks, figuring they'd melt into the dough in the oven. They didn't, and the chocolate chip cookie was born. **WIN!**

TODAY WAS:

❏ Okay   ❏ Lame
❏ Good   ❏ Bad
❏ Awesome   ❏ Super crappy   _____
❏ Epic   ❏ Worst. Day. Ever.   DATE

TODAY'S FAIL:

❏ Average   ❏ EPIC   ❏ Super Mega EPIC   ❏ So EPIC it's a WIN

❏ I / ❏ Who?_____ **DID WHAT?**_____

_____

_____

WHY? ❏ Totally meant to do that   ❏ Drunk
❏ Trying to impress someone   ❏ Just a jackass
❏ Other_____

WILL THE LOSERS INVOLVED HAVE TO:

❏ Go to the hospital?   ❏ Move to a new town?   ❏ Get plastic surgery?
❏ Get therapy?   ❏ Other_____

LESSON LEARNED: _____

_____

❏ NEVER again   ❏ Maybe again   ❏ Do again at first opportunity

👍 TODODAY'S WIN:

☐ Above Average   ☐ Massive   ☐ EPIC   ☐ Super Mega EPIC

☐ I / ☐ Who?_____ **DID WHAT?**_____

_____

_____

WHY? ☐ Totally awesome   ☐ Preparation
         ☐ Deserved it   ☐ Dumb luck
         ☐ Other_____

DID THE WIN RESULT IN A:

☐ New nickname?   ☐ Hookup?   ☐ Trophy?
☐ Arrest?   ☐ Other_____

ALL HAIL_____ , RULER OF_____!
           (winner's name)   (today's win)

If you're racking up a lot more **FAILs** than **WINs**, you may just need to get more sleep. Being awake for twenty hours is equivalent to drinking more than four beers. And a lot less fun.

TODAY WAS:

- ❏ Okay
- ❏ Good
- ❏ Awesome
- ❏ Epic
- ❏ Lame
- ❏ Bad
- ❏ Super crappy
- ❏ Worst. Day. Ever.

_____
DATE

👎 TODAY'S FAIL:

- ❏ Average
- ❏ EPIC
- ❏ Super Mega EPIC
- ❏ So EPIC it's a WIN

❏ I / ❏ Who?_____ **DID WHAT?**_____

_____

_____

WHY?
- ❏ Totally meant to do that
- ❏ Trying to impress someone
- ❏ Other_____
- ❏ Drunk
- ❏ Just a jackass

WILL THE LOSERS INVOLVED HAVE TO:

- ❏ Go to the hospital?
- ❏ Move to a new town?
- ❏ Get plastic surgery?
- ❏ Get therapy?
- ❏ Other_____

LESSON LEARNED: _____

_____

❏ NEVER again   ❏ Maybe again   ❏ Do again at first opportunity

👍 TODAY'S WIN:

☐ Above Average   ☐ Massive   ☐ EPIC   ☐ Super Mega EPIC

☐ I / ☐ Who?_____ **DID WHAT?**_____

_____

_____

WHY?   ☐ Totally awesome   ☐ Preparation
           ☐ Deserved it   ☐ Dumb luck
           ☐ Other_____

DID THE WIN RESULT IN A:

☐ New nickname?   ☐ Hookup?   ☐ Trophy?
☐ Arrest?   ☐ Other_____

ALL HAIL_____ , RULER OF_____ !
         (winner's name)   (today's win)

FAIL⇨WIN: Swiss engineer George de Mestral came home from a walk and found a mess of burrs stuck to his clothes. He examined the burrs under a microscope and thought he might be able to reproduce their stickiness for good. The result? Velcro. **WIN!**

TODAY WAS:

- ❏ Okay
- ❏ Good
- ❏ Awesome
- ❏ Epic

- ❏ Lame
- ❏ Bad
- ❏ Super crappy
- ❏ Worst. Day. Ever.

_____
DATE

👎 TODAY'S FAIL:

❏ Average   ❏ EPIC   ❏ Super Mega EPIC   ❏ So EPIC it's a WIN

❏ I / ❏ Who?_____ **DID WHAT?**_____

_____

_____

WHY?
- ❏ Totally meant to do that
- ❏ Trying to impress someone
- ❏ Other_____

- ❏ Drunk
- ❏ Just a jackass

WILL THE LOSERS INVOLVED HAVE TO:

❏ Go to the hospital?   ❏ Move to a new town?   ❏ Get plastic surgery?
❏ Get therapy?   ❏ Other_____

LESSON LEARNED: _____

_____

❏ NEVER again   ❏ Maybe again   ❏ Do again at first opportunity

👍 TODODAY'S WIN:

☐ Above Average   ☐ Massive   ☐ EPIC   ☐ Super Mega EPIC

☐ I / ☐ Who?_____ **DID WHAT?**_____

_____

_____

WHY? ☐ Totally awesome   ☐ Preparation
         ☐ Deserved it   ☐ Dumb luck
         ☐ Other_____

DID THE WIN RESULT IN A:

☐ New nickname?   ☐ Hookup?   ☐ Trophy?
☐ Arrest?   ☐ Other_____

ALL HAIL _____, RULER OF_____!
        (winner's name)   (today's win)

> *"Success is the ability to go from one failure to another with no loss of enthusiasm."*
>
> **—WINSTON CHURCHILL**

TODAY WAS:

- ❏ Okay
- ❏ Good
- ❏ Awesome
- ❏ Epic
- ❏ Lame
- ❏ Bad
- ❏ Super crappy
- ❏ Worst. Day. Ever.

_____
DATE

👎 TODAY'S FAIL:

❏ Average   ❏ EPIC   ❏ Super Mega EPIC   ❏ So EPIC it's a WIN

❏ I / ❏ Who?_____ **DID WHAT?**_____

_____

_____

WHY?
- ❏ Totally meant to do that
- ❏ Trying to impress someone
- ❏ Other_____
- ❏ Drunk
- ❏ Just a jackass

WILL THE LOSERS INVOLVED HAVE TO:

❏ Go to the hospital?   ❏ Move to a new town?   ❏ Get plastic surgery?
❏ Get therapy?   ❏ Other_____

LESSON LEARNED:_____

_____

❏ NEVER again   ❏ Maybe again   ❏ Do again at first opportunity

👍 TODODAY'S WIN:

❏ Above Average   ❏ Massive   ❏ EPIC   ❏ Super Mega EPIC

❏ I/ ❏ Who?_____ **DID WHAT?**_____

_____

_____

WHY?   ❏ Totally awesome   ❏ Preparation
           ❏ Deserved it   ❏ Dumb luck
           ❏ Other_____

DID THE WIN RESULT IN A:

❏ New nickname?   ❏ Hookup?   ❏ Trophy?
❏ Arrest?   ❏ Other_____

ALL HAIL_____ , RULER OF_____ !
    (winner's name)   (today's win)

> **FAIL⇨WIN:** In 1943, a G.E. engineer named James Wright was
> conducting an experiment with boric acid and silicone oil that resulted
> in a useless blob of goo. Only it turned out not to be so useless after all.
> He'd invented Silly Putty. **WIN!**

TODAY WAS:

❏ Okay ❏ Lame
❏ Good ❏ Bad
❏ Awesome ❏ Super crappy _____
❏ Epic ❏ Worst. Day. Ever. DATE

👎 TODAY'S FAIL:

❏ Average ❏ EPIC ❏ Super Mega EPIC ❏ So EPIC it's a WIN

❏ I / ❏ Who?_____ **DID WHAT?**_____

_____

_____

WHY? ❏ Totally meant to do that ❏ Drunk
❏ Trying to impress someone ❏ Just a jackass
❏ Other_____

WILL THE LOSERS INVOLVED HAVE TO:

❏ Go to the hospital? ❏ Move to a new town? ❏ Get plastic surgery?
❏ Get therapy? ❏ Other_____

LESSON LEARNED: _____

_____

❏ NEVER again ❏ Maybe again ❏ Do again at first opportunity

👍 TODODAY'S WIN:

❏ Above Average ❏ Massive ❏ EPIC ❏ Super Mega EPIC

❏ I / ❏ Who?_____ **DID WHAT?**_____

_____

_____

WHY? ❏ Totally awesome ❏ Preparation
❏ Deserved it ❏ Dumb luck
❏ Other_____

DID THE WIN RESULT IN A:

❏ New nickname? ❏ Hookup? ❏ Trophy?
❏ Arrest? ❏ Other_____

ALL HAIL_____, RULER OF_____!
(winner's name) (today's win)

WIN/FAIL fact: The L to the forehead doesn't mean "loser" everywhere. In the Philippines, it's a political rallying gesture that means "Fight!" **WIN!**

TODAY WAS:

- ❏ Okay
- ❏ Good
- ❏ Awesome
- ❏ Epic
- ❏ Lame
- ❏ Bad
- ❏ Super crappy
- ❏ Worst. Day. Ever.

_____
DATE

👎 TODAY'S FAIL:

❏ Average ❏ EPIC ❏ Super Mega EPIC ❏ So EPIC it's a WIN

❏ I / ❏ Who?_____ **DID WHAT?**_____

_____

_____

WHY?
- ❏ Totally meant to do that
- ❏ Trying to impress someone
- ❏ Other_____
- ❏ Drunk
- ❏ Just a jackass

WILL THE LOSERS INVOLVED HAVE TO:

❏ Go to the hospital? ❏ Move to a new town? ❏ Get plastic surgery?
❏ Get therapy? ❏ Other_____

LESSON LEARNED: _____

_____

❏ NEVER again ❏ Maybe again ❏ Do again at first opportunity

👍 TODODAY'S WIN:

☐ Above Average   ☐ Massive   ☐ EPIC   ☐ Super Mega EPIC

☐ I / ☐ Who?_____ **DID WHAT?**_____

_____

_____

WHY? ☐ Totally awesome   ☐ Preparation
         ☐ Deserved it   ☐ Dumb luck
         ☐ Other_____

DID THE WIN RESULT IN A:

☐ New nickname?   ☐ Hookup?   ☐ Trophy?
☐ Arrest?   ☐ Other_____

ALL HAIL_____, RULER OF_____!
        (winner's name)   (today's win)

WIN/FAIL fact: The V for Victory sign does not mean "victory" everywhere.
In some countries, it means, "Up yours." **FAIL!**

TODAY WAS:

- ❏ Okay
- ❏ Good
- ❏ Awesome
- ❏ Epic
- ❏ Lame
- ❏ Bad
- ❏ Super crappy
- ❏ Worst. Day. Ever.

_____

DATE

👎 TODAY'S FAIL:

❏ Average   ❏ EPIC   ❏ Super Mega EPIC   ❏ So EPIC it's a WIN

❏ I / ❏ Who?_____ **DID WHAT?**_____

_____

_____

WHY?
- ❏ Totally meant to do that
- ❏ Trying to impress someone
- ❏ Other_____
- ❏ Drunk
- ❏ Just a jackass

WILL THE LOSERS INVOLVED HAVE TO:

❏ Go to the hospital?   ❏ Move to a new town?   ❏ Get plastic surgery?
❏ Get therapy?   ❏ Other_____

LESSON LEARNED:_____

_____

❏ NEVER again   ❏ Maybe again   ❏ Do again at first opportunity

👍 TODODAY'S WIN:

☐ Above Average   ☐ Massive   ☐ EPIC   ☐ Super Mega EPIC

☐ I / ☐ Who?_____ **DID WHAT?**_____

_____

_____

WHY? ☐ Totally awesome   ☐ Preparation
          ☐ Deserved it   ☐ Dumb luck
          ☐ Other_____

DID THE WIN RESULT IN A:

☐ New nickname?   ☐ Hookup?   ☐ Trophy?
☐ Arrest?   ☐ Other_____

ALL HAIL_____, RULER OF_____!
         (winner's name)   (today's win)

Schadenfreude is the German word for the feeling of pleasure we get from another's misfortune, and it's what's behind our enjoyment of the **EPIC FAIL.** There is no German word for pleasure in another's win.

TODAY WAS:

- ❏ Okay
- ❏ Good
- ❏ Awesome
- ❏ Epic
- ❏ Lame
- ❏ Bad
- ❏ Super crappy
- ❏ Worst. Day. Ever.

_____
DATE

👎 TODAY'S FAIL:

❏ Average   ❏ EPIC   ❏ Super Mega EPIC   ❏ So EPIC it's a WIN

❏ I / ❏ Who?_____   **DID WHAT?**_____

_____

_____

WHY?
- ❏ Totally meant to do that
- ❏ Trying to impress someone
- ❏ Other_____
- ❏ Drunk
- ❏ Just a jackass

WILL THE LOSERS INVOLVED HAVE TO:

❏ Go to the hospital?   ❏ Move to a new town?   ❏ Get plastic surgery?
❏ Get therapy?   ❏ Other_____

LESSON LEARNED:_____

_____

❏ NEVER again   ❏ Maybe again   ❏ Do again at first opportunity

👍 TODAY'S WIN:

❑ Above Average ❑ Massive ❑ EPIC ❑ Super Mega EPIC

❑ I / ❑ Who?_____ **DID WHAT?**_____

_____

_____

WHY?
❑ Totally awesome ❑ Preparation
❑ Deserved it ❑ Dumb luck
❑ Other_____

DID THE WIN RESULT IN A:

❑ New nickname? ❑ Hookup? ❑ Trophy?
❑ Arrest? ❑ Other_____

ALL HAIL _____ , RULER OF _____ !
(winner's name) (today's win)

FAIL⇨WIN: In 1930, Ruth Wakefield was making a batch of chocolate cookies but didn't have time to melt and blend chocolate into the dough. So she threw in some chocolate chunks, figuring they'd melt into the dough in the oven. They didn't, and the chocolate chip cookie was born. **WIN!**

TODAY WAS:

❑ Okay ❑ Lame
❑ Good ❑ Bad
❑ Awesome ❑ Super crappy
❑ Epic ❑ Worst. Day. Ever.

_____ DATE

👎 TODAY'S FAIL:

❑ Average ❑ EPIC ❑ Super Mega EPIC ❑ So EPIC it's a WIN

❑ I / ❑ Who?_____ **DID WHAT?**_____

_____

_____

WHY? ❑ Totally meant to do that ❑ Drunk
❑ Trying to impress someone ❑ Just a jackass
❑ Other_____

WILL THE LOSERS INVOLVED HAVE TO:

❑ Go to the hospital? ❑ Move to a new town? ❑ Get plastic surgery?
❑ Get therapy? ❑ Other_____

LESSON LEARNED: _____

_____

❑ NEVER again ❑ Maybe again ❑ Do again at first opportunity

👍 TODESY'S WIN:

☐ Above Average ☐ Massive ☐ EPIC ☐ Super Mega EPIC

☐ I / ☐ Who?_____ **DID WHAT?**_____

_____

_____

WHY? ☐ Totally awesome ☐ Preparation
☐ Deserved it ☐ Dumb luck
☐ Other_____

DID THE WIN RESULT IN A:

☐ New nickname? ☐ Hookup? ☐ Trophy?
☐ Arrest? ☐ Other_____

ALL HAIL _____ , RULER OF_____ !
(winner's name) (today's win)

If you're racking up a lot more **FAILs** than **WINs**, you may just need to get more sleep. Being awake for twenty hours is equivalent to drinking more than four beers. And a lot less fun.

TODAY WAS:

- ❏ Okay
- ❏ Good
- ❏ Awesome
- ❏ Epic
- ❏ Lame
- ❏ Bad
- ❏ Super crappy
- ❏ Worst. Day. Ever.

_____
DATE

👎 TODAY'S FAIL:

- ❏ Average
- ❏ EPIC
- ❏ Super Mega EPIC
- ❏ So EPIC it's a WIN

❏ I / ❏ Who?_____ **DID WHAT?**_____

_____

_____

WHY?
- ❏ Totally meant to do that
- ❏ Trying to impress someone
- ❏ Other_____
- ❏ Drunk
- ❏ Just a jackass

WILL THE LOSERS INVOLVED HAVE TO:

- ❏ Go to the hospital?
- ❏ Get therapy?
- ❏ Move to a new town?
- ❏ Other_____
- ❏ Get plastic surgery?

LESSON LEARNED:_____

_____

❏ NEVER again   ❏ Maybe again   ❏ Do again at first opportunity

👍 TODODAY'S WIN:

☐ Above Average   ☐ Massive   ☐ EPIC   ☐ Super Mega EPIC

☐ I / ☐ Who?_____ **DID WHAT?**_____

_____

_____

WHY? ☐ Totally awesome   ☐ Preparation
         ☐ Deserved it   ☐ Dumb luck
         ☐ Other_____

DID THE WIN RESULT IN A:

☐ New nickname?   ☐ Hookup?   ☐ Trophy?
☐ Arrest?   ☐ Other_____

ALL HAIL _____, RULER OF_____!
        (winner's name)   (today's win)

FAIL⇨WIN: Swiss engineer George de Mestral came home from a walk and found a mess of burrs stuck to his clothes. He examined the burrs under a microscope and thought he might be able to reproduce their stickiness for good. The result? Velcro. **WIN!**

TODAY WAS:

❏ Okay ❏ Lame
❏ Good ❏ Bad
❏ Awesome ❏ Super crappy
❏ Epic ❏ Worst. Day. Ever.

_____
DATE

👎 TODAY'S FAIL:

❏ Average ❏ EPIC ❏ Super Mega EPIC ❏ So EPIC it's a WIN

❏ I / ❏ Who?_____ **DID WHAT?**_____

_____

_____

WHY? ❏ Totally meant to do that ❏ Drunk
❏ Trying to impress someone ❏ Just a jackass
❏ Other_____

WILL THE LOSERS INVOLVED HAVE TO:

❏ Go to the hospital? ❏ Move to a new town? ❏ Get plastic surgery?
❏ Get therapy? ❏ Other_____

LESSON LEARNED:_____

_____

❏ NEVER again ❏ Maybe again ❏ Do again at first opportunity

👍 TODALE'S WIN:

☐ Above Average   ☐ Massive   ☐ EPIC   ☐ Super Mega EPIC

☐ I / ☐ Who?_____ **DID WHAT?**_____

_____

_____

WHY? ☐ Totally awesome   ☐ Preparation
☐ Deserved it   ☐ Dumb luck
☐ Other_____

DID THE WIN RESULT IN A:

☐ New nickname?   ☐ Hookup?   ☐ Trophy?
☐ Arrest?   ☐ Other_____

ALL HAIL _____, **RULER OF** _____!
(winner's name)   (today's win)

> *"Success is the ability to go from one failure to another with no loss of enthusiasm."*
>
> **—WINSTON CHURCHILL**

TODAY WAS:

- ❏ Okay
- ❏ Good
- ❏ Awesome
- ❏ Epic
- ❏ Lame
- ❏ Bad
- ❏ Super crappy
- ❏ Worst. Day. Ever.

_____ DATE

👎 TODAY'S FAIL:

- ❏ Average
- ❏ EPIC
- ❏ Super Mega EPIC
- ❏ So EPIC it's a WIN

❏ I / ❏ Who?_____ **DID WHAT?**_____

_____

_____

WHY?
- ❏ Totally meant to do that
- ❏ Trying to impress someone
- ❏ Other_____
- ❏ Drunk
- ❏ Just a jackass

WILL THE LOSERS INVOLVED HAVE TO:

- ❏ Go to the hospital?
- ❏ Get therapy?
- ❏ Move to a new town?
- ❏ Other_____
- ❏ Get plastic surgery?

LESSON LEARNED: _____

_____

❏ NEVER again ❏ Maybe again ❏ Do again at first opportunity

👍 TODAY'S WIN:

☐ Above Average ☐ Massive ☐ EPIC ☐ Super Mega EPIC

☐ I / ☐ Who?_____ **DID WHAT?**_____

_____

WHY? ☐ Totally awesome   ☐ Preparation
          ☐ Deserved it   ☐ Dumb luck
          ☐ Other_____

DID THE WIN RESULT IN A:

☐ New nickname?   ☐ Hookup?   ☐ Trophy?
☐ Arrest?   ☐ Other_____

ALL HAIL_____, RULER OF_____!
        (winner's name)   (today's win)

FAIL⇨WIN: In 1943, a G.E. engineer named James Wright was conducting an experiment with boric acid and silicone oil that resulted in a useless blob of goo. Only it turned out not to be so useless after all. He'd invented Silly Putty. **WIN!**

TODAY WAS:

- ❏ Okay
- ❏ Good
- ❏ Awesome
- ❏ Epic
- ❏ Lame
- ❏ Bad
- ❏ Super crappy
- ❏ Worst. Day. Ever.

_____
DATE

👎 TODAY'S FAIL:

- ❏ Average
- ❏ EPIC
- ❏ Super Mega EPIC
- ❏ So EPIC it's a WIN

❏ I / ❏ Who?_____ **DID WHAT?**_____

_____

_____

WHY?
- ❏ Totally meant to do that
- ❏ Trying to impress someone
- ❏ Other_____
- ❏ Drunk
- ❏ Just a jackass

WILL THE LOSERS INVOLVED HAVE TO:

- ❏ Go to the hospital?
- ❏ Get therapy?
- ❏ Move to a new town?
- ❏ Other_____
- ❏ Get plastic surgery?

LESSON LEARNED:_____

_____

❏ NEVER again ❏ Maybe again ❏ Do again at first opportunity

👍 TODAY'S WIN:

❏ Above Average ❏ Massive ❏ EPIC ❏ Super Mega EPIC

❏ I / ❏ Who?_____ **DID WHAT?**_____

_____

_____

WHY? ❏ Totally awesome ❏ Preparation
❏ Deserved it ❏ Dumb luck
❏ Other_____

DID THE WIN RESULT IN A:

❏ New nickname? ❏ Hookup? ❏ Trophy?
❏ Arrest? ❏ Other_____

ALL HAIL _____ , RULER OF_____ !
(winner's name) (today's win)

WIN/FAIL fact: The L to the forehead doesn't mean "loser" everywhere. In the Philippines, it's a political rallying gesture that means "Fight!" **WIN!**

TODAY WAS:

- ❏ Okay
- ❏ Good
- ❏ Awesome
- ❏ Epic

- ❏ Lame
- ❏ Bad
- ❏ Super crappy
- ❏ Worst. Day. Ever.

_____

DATE

👎 TODAY'S FAIL:

❏ Average   ❏ EPIC   ❏ Super Mega EPIC   ❏ So EPIC it's a WIN

❏ I / ❏ Who?_____ **DID WHAT?**_____

_____

_____

WHY?
- ❏ Totally meant to do that
- ❏ Trying to impress someone
- ❏ Other_____

- ❏ Drunk
- ❏ Just a jackass

WILL THE LOSERS INVOLVED HAVE TO:

❏ Go to the hospital?   ❏ Move to a new town?   ❏ Get plastic surgery?
❏ Get therapy?   ❏ Other_____

LESSON LEARNED: _____

_____

❏ NEVER again   ❏ Maybe again   ❏ Do again at first opportunity

👍 TODAY'S WIN:

❏ Above Average   ❏ Massive   ❏ EPIC   ❏ Super Mega EPIC

❏ I / ❏ Who?_____ **DID WHAT?**_____

_____

_____

WHY? ❏ Totally awesome   ❏ Preparation
          ❏ Deserved it   ❏ Dumb luck
          ❏ Other_____

DID THE WIN RESULT IN A:

❏ New nickname?   ❏ Hookup?   ❏ Trophy?
❏ Arrest?   ❏ Other_____

ALL HAIL_____, RULER OF_____!
      (winner's name)   (today's win)

WIN/FAIL fact: The V for Victory sign does not mean "victory" everywhere.
In some countries, it means, "Up yours." **FAIL!**

TODAY WAS:

- ❏ Okay
- ❏ Good
- ❏ Awesome
- ❏ Epic
- ❏ Lame
- ❏ Bad
- ❏ Super crappy
- ❏ Worst. Day. Ever.

_____
DATE

TODAY'S FAIL:

- ❏ Average
- ❏ EPIC
- ❏ Super Mega EPIC
- ❏ So EPIC it's a WIN

❏ I / ❏ Who?_____ **DID WHAT?**_____

_____

_____

WHY?
- ❏ Totally meant to do that
- ❏ Trying to impress someone
- ❏ Other_____
- ❏ Drunk
- ❏ Just a jackass

WILL THE LOSERS INVOLVED HAVE TO:

- ❏ Go to the hospital?
- ❏ Get therapy?
- ❏ Move to a new town?
- ❏ Other_____
- ❏ Get plastic surgery?

LESSON LEARNED: _____

_____

❏ NEVER again   ❏ Maybe again   ❏ Do again at first opportunity

👍 TODAY'S WIN:

☐ Above Average ☐ Massive ☐ EPIC ☐ Super Mega EPIC

☐ I / ☐ Who?_____ **DID WHAT?**_____

_____

_____

WHY? ☐ Totally awesome ☐ Preparation
☐ Deserved it ☐ Dumb luck
☐ Other_____

DID THE WIN RESULT IN A:

☐ New nickname? ☐ Hookup? ☐ Trophy?
☐ Arrest? ☐ Other_____

ALL HAIL _____ , RULER OF _____ !
(winner's name)   (today's win)

Schadenfreude is the German word for the feeling of pleasure we get from another's misfortune, and it's what's behind our enjoyment of the **EPIC FAIL.** There is no German word for pleasure in another's win.